Excel

SPREADSHEET APPLICATIONS SERIES

for Accounting Principles

Gaylord N. Smith, CPA

Professor, Albion College, Albion Michigan

 South-Western College Publishing
an International Thomson Publishing company I(T)P®

Cincinnati • Albany • Boston • Detroit • Johannesburg • London • Madrid • Melbourne • Mexico City
New York • Pacific Grove • San Francisco • Scottsdale • Singapore • Tokyo • Toronto

Accounting Team Director: Richard Lindgren
Acquisitions Editor: Rochelle J. Kronzek
Developmental Editor: Rebecca Glaab
Marketing Manager: Matt Filimonov
Media Production Editor: Lora Craver
Cover Design: Rick Moore
Cover Images: © 1998, PhotoDisc, Inc.
Production Editor: Mike Busam

Copyright © 2000
by South-Western College Publishing
Cincinnati, Ohio

I⟨T⟩P®

International Thomson Publishing
South-Western College Publishing is an ITP Company.
The ITP trademark is used under license.

3 4 5 6 GP 4 3 2 1 0

ISBN: 0-538-83421-8

Printed in the United States of America

Smith, Gaylord N.
    Excel spreadsheet applications series for accounting principles /
  Gaylord N. Smith.
        p.   cm.
    Includes index.
    ISBN 0-538-83421-8
    1. Microsoft Excel for Windows. 2. Accounting—Data processing. 3. Electronic
spreadsheets. I. Title
HF5548.4.M523S652 1999
657.'.0285'5369—dc21

                                                                99-24857

CONTENTS

MODEL-BUILDING PROBLEM CHECKLIST   169

MODEL-BUILDING PROBLEMS

MODEL-BUILDING CASES

PREFACE

Flexibility, power, and basic simplicity all combine to make spreadsheet programs very popular in today's business world. The most common uses of spreadsheet programs are for:

- budgeting and financial planning
- financial management and investment analysis
- preparation of financial statements, reports, and graphs
- performance of what-if analysis
- business documents such as invoices, customer statements, and expense reports

In addition to these uses, there are many other applications for spreadsheet programs: depreciation schedules, inventory control, tax planning and preparation, consolidations, statistical analysis, bookkeeping, and so forth.

The purpose of the *Excel Spreadsheet Applications Series* is to bring this technology into the classroom. The series is designed to allow accounting and finance students to learn about and use a computer spreadsheet program along with their normal class assignments. Each workbook in the series contains more than 50 typical homework problems which have been restructured so that they can be solved using a spreadsheet program called Excel for Windows. The workbooks are generic in nature and may be used with any standard textbook in each specific area of accounting.

This series allows students to experience the excitement of working with the sophisticated software that is being used in the real world. It is important to realize that this is not computer-assisted instruction in which the computer catches all the errors, does all the computations, and prints out the answer. Although every effort has been made to provide adequate guidance, it is up to students to develop the final solutions and tell the computer what to do. In completing the problems, students are stretching their knowledge of accounting concepts and learning to use a valuable software tool.

This workbook consists of sample problems, preprogrammed problems, model-building problems, and model-building cases. The student disk that accompanies this workbook contains the files you will need for Sample Problem A, the preprogrammed problems, and the model-building cases.

SAMPLE PROBLEMS

The workbook begins with four sample problems (A, B, C, and D) introducing students to the methodology for solving the three types of workbook problems. Students must complete the sample problems before attempting the corresponding workbook problems.

PREPROGRAMMED PROBLEMS

Problems are included for most of the conceptual areas covered in each specific accounting course. Students develop formulas and enter data to complete partially constructed spreadsheet models. After the basic solution is developed, students perform what-if analyses and interpret graphical information. All preprogrammed problems have optional sections (called ticklers) that stretch students' knowledge of Excel including:

- redesigning and expanding the original model (Worksheet tickler)
- creating additional charts and printing them (Chart tickler)

MODEL-BUILDING PROBLEMS

Short problems from a wide variety of accounting topics are provided to give students experience in developing their own models. No computer files are provided for these problems. Two sets of data are included for each problem so students can build the model with one set and test their model with the other. An optional section of each problem challenges students to create a chart from the data.

CASES

Cases are distinguished from model-building problems in two ways: (1) cases utilize extensive data and require lengthy solutions and (2) the data for each case is collected in a spreadsheet file on the Student Disk. Like the model-building problems, cases include two sets of data and have an optional section with a chart assignment.

SEPARATE TUTORIAL AND REFERENCE BOOK

Some students have been introduced to Excel elsewhere, while other students are encountering this spreadsheet program for the first time. The *Excel Spreadsheet Applications Series* is structured for success for all students regardless of prior experience.

A separate tutorial and reference book called *Excel Quick* by Gaylord Smith is specifically designed for users of the *Excel Spreadsheet Applications Series*. The tutorial introduces the basics of using Excel. Although it is not the purpose of this tutorial to teach extensive spreadsheet programming, it does cover all the basic commands thoroughly, including charts and business functions, and it introduces a few important frills.

Each of the five lessons in the tutorial takes between 30 and 60 minutes to complete.

Lesson 1 - Covers entering text and numbers, editing entries, changing column widths, using toolbar buttons (italic, bold, align, underline, undo, sum, and borders), saving, and printing worksheets.

Lesson 2 - Covers arithmetic calculations, number formats, designing formulas, using Excel functions, and displaying cell contents.

Lesson 3 - Covers copying data, moving data, inserting and deleting new columns and rows, and centering data across columns.

Lesson 4 - Covers global settings, special date formats, using the fill handle, establishing standard column widths, using accounting underlines, protecting cells and worksheets, naming cells and ranges, freezing columns and rows, using multiple worksheets at once, and adding artwork to worksheets.

Lesson 5 - Covers creating charts, modifying and changing charts, enhancing charts with special features, using chart sheets, saving, and printing charts.

Appendix A - Built-in Excel functions for business applications.

Appendix B - Model-building hints.

Appendix C - Simple, real world applications using Excel.

Although it is highly recommended, it is not required that *Excel Quick* be used with this workbook.

BENEFITS TO STUDENTS USING THIS SERIES

The focus of this series is to facilitate spreadsheet use as an integral part of the accounting curriculum. This workbook builds on the success of earlier editions written for versions of Lotus 1-2-3 and Quattro Pro. Among the advantages to instructors and students of using this workbook are:

1. **Variety of what-if analyses.** Solutions to textbook problems generally result in a single answer. Solving textbook problems with a pencil and paper is generally quicker than typing everything into a spreadsheet model. So why waste time and energy just for the thrill of using a spreadsheet program? The answer lies in the spreadsheet's ability to perform what-if analysis. All the problems in this workbook utilize the tremendous what-if capabilities of spreadsheet programs to go beyond a single solution.

   After students develop the initial answer, they are asked a number of what-if questions. As a result, the spreadsheet models in the workbook are not only used to solve homework problems, they also reinforce the accounting concepts being taught in the classroom and they provide a demonstration of the instantaneous recalculative power of the spreadsheet program. As a result, the computer's capabilities are being *productively* used by students.

2. **Use of charts.** All problems in this workbook have optional chart assignments. Students are asked to interpret charts, create charts, print charts, and perform what-if charting. Charts are an increasingly important part of financial communications, and this workbook is unique in the special emphasis placed on it.

3.   **Classroom tested tutorial.** The basic five-lesson tutorial in *Excel Quick* that introduces students to the world of Excel has been tested extensively in the classroom. Students are led through the Excel program in an efficient, step-by-step fashion. When students complete the tutorial, they will be prepared to work with existing models and to develop some reasonably sophisticated models of their own.

4.   **Sound pedagogy.** In the design of the workbook series, much attention has been given to supporting and enhancing the learning process. The learning process begins with a tutorial and sample problems that provide a sound foundation for completing the workbook problems. The preprogrammed problems require students to use accounting concepts to solve problems with partially completed models. The model-building problems and the cases challenge students to use accounting concepts and their knowledge of Excel to design their own models.

Check figures are included for every problem. Appendices in *Excel Quick* provide useful information on functions for business and model-building hints. A particularly useful appendix provides several examples of Excel models that can be utilized in business.

INSTRUCTOR RESOURCES

Instructors adopting a workbook from this series will be provided with a solution disk and an instructor's manual. The disk contains solutions to all parts of the preprogrammed problems and suggested designs for the model-building problems and cases. The manual provides all formulas and written answers required of the students, as well as all required printouts. The manual also contains suggestions on how to integrate the spreadsheet problems into the course, as well as other resource material.

ACKNOWLEDGEMENTS

I wish to express my sincere appreciation to the many users of earlier editions of this workbook who have offered helpful suggestions. Colleagues in the teaching profession have been generous in contributing to the ongoing improvement of this workbook, and I thank you all.

I would like to acknowledge the excellent support I have received from the sales, editorial, and production staff at South-Western. Their commitment to the highest standards of quality and professionalism have made my association with them a pleasure.

This workbook represents an attempt to carefully combine the teaching of accounting with a well-planned, valuable exposure to spreadsheets. I hope I have succeeded in my objective. Any comments, criticisms, or suggestions that you have regarding the workbook, its goals, and its organization are openly solicited and welcomed.

GAYLORD N. SMITH
Department of Economics and Management
Albion College, Albion, MI 49224
gsmith@albion.edu

INSTRUCTIONS FOR SAMPLE PROBLEMS

There are three sets of problems contained in this workbook: preprogrammed, model-building, and cases. With the preprogrammed problems, you will complete spreadsheet worksheets that have already been set up for you. You must finish the worksheet, experiment with the results, and then answer several questions to complete each assignment. The basic instructions for completing preprogrammed problems are found in Sample Problem A.

Each preprogrammed problem has two optional sections at the end—a Worksheet Tickler and a Chart Tickler. Solving the ticklers involves using spreadsheet commands to physically alter the appearance and/or components of the current model. In order to solve the Worksheet Ticklers, you will need some familiarity with spreadsheet modeling concepts and a basic understanding of spreadsheet commands. A sample Worksheet Tickler is shown in Sample Problem B. Sample Problem C serves as preparation for the Chart Ticklers.

With the model-building problems and the cases, you must develop models from start to finish. Model-building problems are generally not complex, but they take as long to complete as the preprogrammed problems because you have to design the whole worksheet model yourself. Cases are usually long, complicated problems and require substantial effort to complete. Sample Problem D contains a worked-out example of a model-building problem and includes hints for completing both the model-building problems and the cases.

As the following table illustrates, you must have some knowledge of Excel before attempting the sample problems. It is highly recommended that the book *Excel Quick* written by Gaylord Smith specifically for users of South-Western College Publishing's *Excel Spreadsheet Applications Series* be used for this purpose.

| | Preparatory Materials | |
Workbook Problems	*Excel Quick* Lessons	Workbook Sample Problems
Preprogrammed	Lessons 1 and 2	Sample Problem A
Worksheet Tickler	Lessons 3 and 4	Sample Problem B
Chart Tickler	Lesson 5	Sample Problem C
Model-building and Cases	Lessons 1-4 (Lesson 5 optional)	Sample Problem D

Sample Problem A

SAMPLE PREPROGRAMMED PROBLEM

This sample problem is designed to acquaint you with the procedures used to solve the preprogrammed problems in this workbook. Each problem covers a different conceptual area in accounting. The problems are equivalent in length to standard accounting homework problems. Initially the problems may require a little more time than regular homework since you still may be somewhat unfamiliar with your spreadsheet program. Once you begin to feel more comfortable, your problem assignments should go quicker.

Before attempting Sample Problem A, you must have certain fundamental skills in Excel. You must be able to enter text and numbers, modify or delete entries, save and print files, use Excel to perform arithmetic calculations, use Excel functions, and design formulas using cell references. These skills are covered in Lessons 1 and 2 of *Excel Quick*, a tutorial by Gaylord Smith specifically written for users of South-Western College Publishing's *Excel Spreadsheet Applications Series*.

The Student Disk provided with this workbook contains a spreadsheet file for each preprogrammed problem. Each file contains a worksheet that is generally divided into two sections—a Data Section and an Answer Section. The Data Section contains the quantitative information needed to solve the problem. The Answer Section provides the basic format for your solution.

The preprogrammed problems have the following parts: the problem statement, the problem requirements, a printout of the worksheet file, and the file itself which is found on the Student Disk. The general procedures for solving the problems will be explained in the following paragraphs, using a sample problem. The sample problem appears in the boxed areas on the following pages.

First, read the problem statement shown in Illustration SP-1. The word SAMPLE in parentheses indicates the name of the file on the Student Disk for this problem. *Do not* open the file yet.

S1 ☆ FINANCIAL PROJECTIONS (SAMPLE)

PROBLEM DATA

Ecosys International is interested in estimating its net income for each of the next five months. It appears that January sales will be $10,000, and the company is hopeful that sales will increase by 2% per month. Selling expenses are roughly 60% of each month's sales, and general expenses average $1,900 each month.

Illustration SP-1   *Sample Problem Statement*

Next, read the first problem requirement shown in Illustration SP-2. This requirement states the basic aim of the problem and asks you to review the printout of the worksheet.

REQUIRED

1)   You have been asked by Ecosys International to provide net income projections for the next five months. Review the printout of the worksheet called SAMPLE. Note that the problem data have already been entered into the Data Section of the worksheet. Note also that the basic format for the solution has been set up in the Answer Section.

Illustration SP-2   *Sample Problem Requirement 1*

A printout of the worksheet is found at the end of each problem. The worksheet printout for the sample problem is shown in Illustration SP-3.

Notice the following features of the worksheet:

1.　　In the upper center of the worksheet, you will see the file name SAMPLE. You should always check the file name to see that you have opened the correct file from the Student Disk.
2.　　The work area of the worksheet is divided into two sections—the Data Section and the Answer Section.
3.　　The Answer Section contains several cells labeled FORMULA1, FORMULA2, etc. This indicates the cells in which you will be entering your formulas to solve the problem.

The next step is to write the formulas. Requirement 2, shown in Illustration SP-4, asks you to develop the necessary formulas. The formulas and comments on each are shown after the illustration. Use the information in the Data Section of the worksheet to develop these formulas. Wherever possible, formulas should incorporate cell addresses rather than specific values. The importance of this will be seen when you perform the what-if analysis in requirement 4. Write the formulas in the spaces provided in Illustration SP-4.

Illustration SP-4   *Sample Problem Requirement 2*

The formulas for the sample problems are below.

FORMULA1: **=D7**

Comment on Formula 1: January sales are given in cell D7 in the Data Section. This formula tells the program to use the value found in cell D7 as January sales in the Answer Section of the worksheet.

FORMULA2: **=D7*(1+D8) or =D7+D7*D8 or =B15*(1+D8)**

Comment on Formula 2: Any of these formulas will do. These formulas will calculate February sales as a 2% increase over January sales. March, April, and May sales are already preprogrammed in the worksheet. Note that you have expressed the growth rate as a cell address (D8). This allows you to change the growth rate simply by changing the number in cell D8 rather than by redoing the formula in cell C15. What-if analysis with different growth rates can be performed very quickly this way.

FORMULA3: **=D7*D9 or =B15*D9**

Comment on Formula 3: According to the problem statement, selling expenses are 60% of sales. Since January sales are already given in cell D7 (or cell B15) and the selling expense ratio is given in cell D9, you can simply multiply the two to compute total selling expenses for the month of January.

FORMULA4: **=D10**

Comment on Formula 4: General expenses are given in the Data Section in cell D10. This formula tells the program to take the value found in cell D10 and place it in cell B18.

FORMULA5:   =B17+B18 or =SUM(B17:B18)

Comment on Formula 5: Total expenses are the sum of the selling and general expenses. The =SUM function is frequently used in Excel models.

FORMULA6:   =B15-B19

Comment on Formula 6: Net income is the difference between sales and total expenses.

After you have written the formulas in the workbook, the next requirement will ask you to start the spreadsheet program, open the proper worksheet file, and enter the required information. You are also asked to enter your name, save your solution and print your completed file. Read requirement 3 shown in Illustration SP-5.

---

3)   Start the spreadsheet program and open the file SAMPLE from the Student Disk. Enter the six formulas in the appropriate cells. Enter your name in cell A1. Save your solution as SAMPLE3. Print the worksheet. *Check figure: January net income (cell B20), $2,100*

Illustration SP-5   *Sample Problem Requirement 3*

Follow the steps listed below to complete this requirement.

1.   Start the Excel program and insert the disk that accompanies your workbook in your computer's disk drive (usually drive A). Open the file SAMPLE from the Student Disk.
2.   Check the file name printed in the center of the heading to make sure you have opened the correct file. If you have opened the wrong file, close the incorrect file and try again.
3.   Notice that there are two sheet tabs at the bottom of the worksheet. One is called Worksheet and the other is called Chart. You will always begin your work on the Worksheet. Later you will use the Chart sheet. In fact in most cases, the chart on the Chart sheet will look weird until you have completed the worksheet.

4.   Enter the six formulas required to complete the worksheet. All the cells that already have numbers or zeros in them have been preprogrammed with the correct formulas. To enter the required formulas, move to the appropriate cells and type the formulas you wrote in requirement 2. For example, to enter FORMULA1, move to cell B15 and type **=D7**. As you type these formulas, you will see the rest of the worksheet fill in with numbers. When you have entered these formulas, the result should be as shown in Illustration SP-6.

	A	B	C	D	E	F
1	Student Name					
2			SAMPLE			
3			Sample Preprogrammed Problem			
4						
5	Data Section					
6						
7		January sales		$10,000		
8		Sales growth rate		2%		
9		Selling expense ratio		60%		
10		General expenses		$1,900		
11						
12	Answer Section					
13						
14		Jan	Feb	Mar	Apr	May
15	Sales	$10,000	$10,200	$10,404	$10,612	$10,824
16	Expenses					
17	Selling expenses	$6,000	$6,120	$6,242	$6,367	$6,495
18	General expenses	1,900	1,900	1,900	1,900	1,900
19	Total expenses	$7,900	$8,020	$8,142	$8,267	$8,395
20	Net income	$2,100	$2,180	$2,262	$2,345	$2,430
21						

Illustration SP-6   *Screen Display of Completed Model*

5. Check figures are provided for all preprogrammed problems. The check figure for SAMPLE, requirement 3, is January net income, $2,100. Verify that it agrees with your worksheet.
6. Move to cell A1 and enter your name.
7. Save your completed file now under the file name SAMPLE3. To do this, select the File Save As command and enter the file name **SAMPLE3**. Make sure the drive is properly specified for your Student Disk (usually drive A) and then click OK.

WARNING: If you are using Excel 97, you may receive the following message:

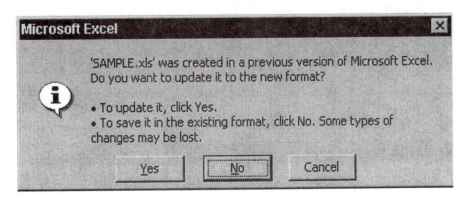

The spreadsheet files in this workbook were originally saved using Excel 5.0/95. If you wish to update this file for Excel 97, click "Yes." Otherwise, click "No." Nothing is "lost" under either format. *All workbook files work equally well under either format.*

Occasionally you may see the following "warning:"

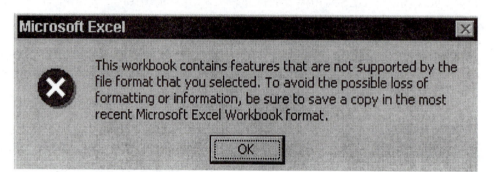

Just click OK. Everything works.

A word about using the file name SAMPLE3. If you had saved the file as SAMPLE instead of SAMPLE3, you would have wiped out the original file. This would cause no huge problem, but if you had really messed up SAMPLE3, you could at least go back to the original SAMPLE and start over.

If you run out of room on your Student Disk to save additional files, you may wish to delete some unneeded files from the disk. For example, the SAMPLE files may be deleted after all of the sample problems are done. Also, each original preprogrammed problem file can be deleted after the initial solution file has been developed, debugged, and saved.

8. To print the file, you will use the normal print commands. Long files will print on appropriately spaced pages without any special instructions from you. Also, worksheets will print with row and column headers showing.

The next section of each problem is called "What-If Analysis." Illustration SP-7 shows the what-if analysis stated in requirement 4 of the sample problem.

WHAT-IF ANALYSIS

4) The two options appearing below are being considered to improve the company's monthly net income over the next five months. Evaluate the effect on net income for each of these options. Consider each case separately. After evaluating each suggestion, enter the monthly projected net income in the spaces provided below. Assume that both options can be accomplished immediately.

OPTION A: Increase the sales commission rate. This means that sales personnel will receive higher commissions when sales are made. This will increase the selling expense ratio to 70%, but it is also expected to increase the sales growth rate from 2 to 5% per month.

OPTION B: Take some salespeople off commissions and put them on a straight salary. As a result of this, it is expected that the selling expense ratio will drop to 50%, but general expenses will increase from $1,900 to $2,900 per month. Also, the sales growth rate will drop to 1% per month.

PROJECTED MONTHLY NET INCOME

	January	February	March	April	May
OPTION A	_____	_____	_____	_____	_____
OPTION B	_____	_____	_____	_____	_____

Recommendation:

Illustration SP-7   *Sample What-If Analysis Requirement*

This what-if question asks you to assess the effect of changes to the original data. The ease with which you will be able to manipulate the problem data and assess the impact on the problem results is an important part of understanding the power and flexibility of spreadsheet programs. This is the main reason for setting up a separate Data Section for most problems and for structuring the formulas using cell references wherever possible.

To explore Option A, move to cell D8 and change it to **.05**. Then move to cell D9 and enter **.7**. The worksheet should appear as shown in Illustration SP-8.

	A	B	C	D	E	F
1	Student Name					
2			*SAMPLE*			
3			*Sample Preprogrammed Problem*			
4						
5	Data Section					
6						
7			January sales	$10,000		
8			Sales growth rate	5%		
9			Selling expense ratio	70%		
10			General expenses	$1,900		
11						
12	Answer Section					
13						
14		Jan	Feb	Mar	Apr	May
15	Sales	$10,000	$10,500	$11,025	$11,576	$12,155
16	Expenses					
17	Selling expenses	$7,000	$7,350	$7,718	$8,103	$8,509
18	General expenses	1,900	1,900	1,900	1,900	1,900
19	Total expenses	$8,900	$9,250	$9,618	$10,003	$10,409
20	Net income	$1,100	$1,250	$1,408	$1,573	$1,747
21						

Illustration SP-8   *Screen Display for Option A*

Note that if the growth rate and selling expense ratio had not been separately listed in the Data Section, you would have had to change several formulas to analyze Option A. Instead, all you had to do was change two numbers!

In the space provided in Illustration SP-7, write the monthly net incomes. Refer to your printout from requirement 3 to see if the results are better or worse than the original projection.

To assess Option B, move to cell D8 and change it to **.01**. Move to cell D9 and change it to **.5**. Finally, move to cell D10 and change it to **2900**. Write your answers in the space provided in Illustration SP-7. The results of Option B should appear as shown in Illustration SP-9.

	A	B	C	D	E	F
1	Student Name					
2			SAMPLE			
3			Sample Preprogrammed Problem			
4						
5	Data Section					
6						
7		January sales		$10,000		
8		Sales growth rate		1%		
9		Selling expense ratio		50%		
10		General expenses		$2,900		
11						
12	Answer Section					
13						
14		Jan	Feb	Mar	Apr	May
15	Sales	$10,000	$10,100	$10,201	$10,303	$10,406
16	Expenses					
17	Selling expenses	$5,000	$5,050	$5,101	$5,152	$5,203
18	General expenses	2,900	2,900	2,900	2,900	2,900
19	Total expenses	$7,900	$7,950	$8,001	$8,052	$8,103
20	Net income	$2,100	$2,150	$2,201	$2,252	$2,303
21						

Illustration SP-9   *Screen Display for Option B*

What is your recommendation regarding these two options? Write your answer in the space provided in Illustration SP-7. Your written answer would be roughly as follows: Given the worksheet results, it seems clear that neither of these two options improves the company's net income projection for the next five months, and both should be rejected.

Your instructor may require you to print the file for each of the what-if scenarios. You will use normal print commands to do this.

The final requirement of each problem is a section entitled "Graphical Analysis." Requirement 5 of the sample preprogrammed problem is shown in Illustration SP-10. To begin solving this requirement, you are asked to reset the Data Section to its initial values. To do this, set cell D8 to **.02**, cell D9 to **.6**, and cell D10 to **1900**. Then click the Chart sheet tab. Immediately you will be moved to the second sheet in the SAMPLE3 file and will see the line chart shown in Illustration SP-11.

GRAPHICAL ANALYSIS

5)   Reset the Data Section to its initial values and click the Chart sheet tab. A chart appears on the screen indicating the relationship between sales and total expenses over the five-month period. The gap between sales and total expenses is net income.

A common interest of managers is a company's break-even point. This is the sales volume at which a company's dollar sales are equal to its total expenses. At the break-even point, net income is zero. Only when a company operates above the break-even point will it have profits. Use the chart to find Ecosys International's break-even point and enter the amount below.

Break-even sales $_____

HINT: Find a January sales level (cell D7 on the Worksheet) which causes the two lines to cross. The point at which the two lines cross is the break-even point.

When the assignment is complete, close the file without saving it again.

Illustration SP-10   *Sample Graphical Analysis Requirement*

Notice that the sales line is above the total expense line. Thus, with a January sales volume of $10,000, Ecosys International will earn a positive net income each month because sales are greater than total expenses.

Click the Worksheet sheet tab to return to the worksheet and enter **8000** in cell D7. Click the Chart sheet tab again. Notice that the sales and total expenses lines are closer together, but they do not cross. Try different values in cell D7 on the worksheet and check the chart after each try until you get the lines to cross.

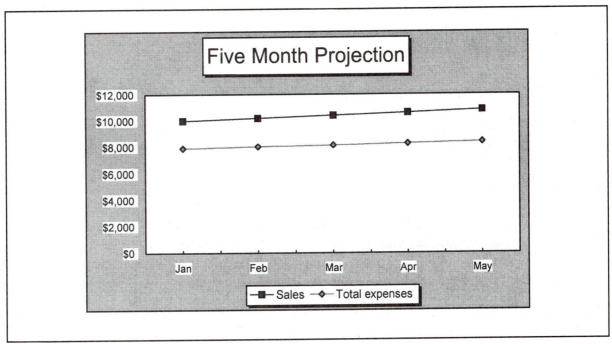

Illustration SP-11   *Line Chart*

A January sales level between $4,400 and $4,750 will result in the sales and total expenses lines crossing on the screen. As you read the chart, you will see that the break-even point is sales of $4,750. At this level of sales, net income is zero. You should now write this answer in the space provided in Illustration SP-10.

You have now completed the sample preprogrammed problem. Your final instruction is to close the SAMPLE3 file without saving it again. Do that now.

You may erase the file SAMPLE from your Student Disk to make more room for other preprogrammed problem solution files. **You must keep the file SAMPLE3 on your Student Disk because it is needed for the sample tickler problems that follow.**

Sample Problem B

SAMPLE WORKSHEET TICKLER

The final part of the preprogrammed problems are the ticklers. These are optional sections that differ from the rest of the problem in that their solutions involve altering the worksheet itself. There are two ticklers for the problems—a Worksheet Tickler and a Chart Tickler. The Worksheet Tickler is covered in Sample Problem B and the Chart Tickler is covered in Sample Problem C.

Before attempting the sample Worksheet Tickler, you must have certain skills in Excel. You should be able to copy and move data, insert and delete rows and columns, change column widths, use a wide variety of Toolbar buttons, use the fill handle, freeze panes, and add artwork spreadsheet models. These skills are covered in Lessons 3 and 4 of *Excel Quick*, a tutorial by Gaylord Smith specifically written for users of South-Western College Publishing's *Excel Spreadsheet Applications Series*. You also need to have completed the sample preprogrammed problem (Sample Problem A).

The purpose of Worksheet Ticklers is to demonstrate to you that the workbook files are not carved in stone and that they may be readily adapted to different facts and circumstances. The Worksheet Tickler for the sample preprogrammed problem is shown in Illustration SP-12. After you worked through Sample Problem A, you saved your answer as file SAMPLE3. Open that file now.

TICKLERS (optional)

Worksheet. Late in December, Ecosys International had to obtain a bank loan to pay some business debts. The interest expense for this loan will amount to $300 per month. Alter the SAMPLE3 worksheet to include Interest expense as an additional input item in the Data Section and also include the interest as an additional expense in the Answer Section (put it under General expenses). Put your name in cell A1. Use the Print Preview command (File menu) to make sure that the worksheet will print neatly on one page, then print the worksheet. Save the completed file as SAMPLET.

Illustration SP-12   *Sample Problem Worksheet Tickler*

After opening the file, you must unprotect it. To do this, select the Protection command (Tools menu), and choose the Unprotect Sheet option.

The Worksheet Tickler asks you to insert an additional expense into the model. To add the additional expense to the Data Section, move to row 11 and insert a new row (Rows command [Insert menu]). In cell B11, enter **Interest expense**. Then enter **300** in cell D11.

Notice that the $300 in cell D11 is already properly formatted and unprotected. When you use the Insert Rows command, new rows will have the same formatting as the row just above the insertion.

To alter the Answer Section, use the following steps:

1. Move to row 20 (old row 19) and insert a new row (Insert Rows command) under General expenses.
2. Once again the Insert command has copied styles to the new row. The underlines in row 19 have been copied to row 20. To get rid of the underlines in row 19, select the range B19 to F19. Then click the Borders button and choose the border style that has no borders (upper left corner option).

Borders

3. In cell A20, press the SPACEBAR five times and enter **Interest expense**.
4. In cell B20, enter the formula **=$D11** (or type **+** and point to D11 and press **F4** [ABS] three times). The $ is needed for step 5 since you want the D in D11 to be absolute. Again, note that the cell is already properly formatted.
5. Copy the formula in cell B20 to cells C20 through F20. To do this, select cell B20 and click the Copy button. Then select the range C20 to F20 and click the Paste button. Notice that the gray shading in cell B20 is also copied. This can be cleaned up later.

Copy   Paste

6. Modify the total expenses formula for January using either of the following formulas:

B21:+B18+B19+B20 or **=SUM(B18.B20)**

7. Copy the total expense formula for January to the other cells in that row using the Copy and Paste buttons.
8. If you wish to remove the gray shading in the copied cells, first select the range of cells from C20 to F21. Then choose the Cells command (Format menu) and click the Patterns tab. Pick the No Color option and click OK.

9. If you wish to change the bold, blue font in the copied cells, select the range of cells from C20 to F21. Then choose the Cells command (Format menu) and click the Font tab. Pick the color Black and the Font Style Regular. Then click OK.

10. Type your name in cell A1.

When you are done, the worksheet should appear as shown in Illustration SP-13.

	A	B	C	D	E	F
1	Student Name					
2		SAMPLE				
3		Sample Preprogrammed Problem				
4						
5	Data Section					
6						
7		January sales		$10,000		
8		Sales growth rate		2%		
9		Selling expense ratio		60%		
10		General expenses		$1,900		
11		Interest expense		$300		
12						
13	Answer Section					
14						
15		Jan	Feb	Mar	Apr	May
16	Sales	$10,000	$10,200	$10,404	$10,612	$10,824
17	Expenses					
18	Selling expenses	$6,000	$6,120	$6,242	$6,367	$6,495
19	General expenses	1,900	1,900	1,900	1,900	1,900
20	Interest espense	300	300	300	300	300
21	Total expenses	$8,200	$8,320	$8,442	$8,567	$8,695
22	Net income	$1,800	$1,880	$1,962	$2,045	$2,130
23						

Illustration SP-13   *Completed Worksheet Tickler*

To reprotect your altered worksheet, select the Protection command (Tools menu) and choose the Protect Sheet option.

To avoid wasting paper on an improperly spaced printout, you should preview the printout before printing it. Select the Print Preview command (File Menu) to view your file now. With this particular Worksheet Tickler, the modifications do not significantly alter the page layout so you will see that the revised model will print neatly on one page. If you do encounter a case where the modified printout appears to be sloppy (e.g., stray columns of numbers, etc.), you can clean it up using forced page breaks.

Print the worksheet now using normal print commands.

Save your modified masterpiece using the file name SAMPLET (File Save As).

After your instructor has reviewed your work, you may delete SAMPLET to create more room on your Student Disk for future homework files. **You must keep SAMPLE3 on your disk for the Chart Tickler (Sample Problem C).**

Sample Problem C

SAMPLE CHART TICKLER

The purpose of Chart Ticklers is to introduce the various charting options available in the spreadsheet program. Before attempting the sample Chart Tickler, you must have certain skills in Excel. You should be able to create and modify a basic chart, move it, resize it, print it, and save it. These skills are covered in Lesson 5 of *Excel Quick*, a tutorial by Gaylord Smith specifically written for users of South-Western College Publishing's *Excel Spreadsheet Applications Series*. You also need to have completed the sample preprogrammed problem (Sample Problem A).

The Chart Tickler for the sample preprogrammed problem is shown in Illustration SP-14.

Chart. Using the SAMPLE3 file, prepare a chart that shows what happened to May's sales revenue (i.e., the percentage spent for selling expenses, general expenses, and the amount left over for net income). Complete the Chart Tickler Data Table and use it as a basis for preparing the chart. Put your name somewhere on the chart. Save the modified file as SAMPLE3 again. Print the chart.

Illustration SP-14　　　*Sample Problem Chart Tickler*

To begin the tickler, open SAMPLE3 from your Student Disk and do the following:

1.　　After opening the file, click the Chart sheet tab and press the PgDn key. If the problem you are working on uses a Chart Tickler Data Table, this is where it will always be. To complete this table, the range E24 to E26 needs to be filled in based on data from the worksheet. Generally you can enter either formulas or the values themselves. You are encouraged to enter formulas wherever possible since this will maximize your chart's what-if potential.
2.　　Click in cell E24. Before working on this sheet, you must unprotect it. To do this, select the Protection command (Tools menu), and select the Unprotect Sheet option.
3.　　Now that the sheet is unprotected, in cell E24 press the = (equal sign), click the Worksheet tab, select cell F17, and press ENTER. This places the formula =Worksheet!F17 in cell E24 and the value $6,495 should appear.
　　　　Next, repeat this process to enter **=Worksheet!F18** in cell E25 and **=Worksheet!F20** in cell E26. Your completed Chart Tickler Data Table should appear as shown in Illustration SP-15.

	A	B	C	D	E	F
19						
20						
21						
22				Chart Tickler		
23				Data Table		
24				Selling	$6,495	
25				General	1,900	
26				Net income	$2,430	
27						

Illustration SP-15   *Sample Chart Tickler Data Table*

4.   Select the range D24 to E26 and click the Chart Wizard button.

5.   **Excel 5.0 and Excel 95.** Now you need to position your new chart. Point to cell B23, hold down the mouse button and drag over an area down to cell G34. Release the mouse button. Then complete the following five steps. Step 1—Click Next. Step 2—Line charts are recommended for showing behaviors over a time period, bar charts are good for comparing different items at the same point in time, and pie charts are used to show the relative proportion of elements that make up a whole. A pie chart is what you want in this tickler. Pick the 3-D Pie chart and click Next. Step 3—Pick sub-type #6. This option will place percents as data labels on the face of the chart. Click Next. Step 4—Click Next. Step 5—Click Yes to Add a Legend. Also, enter **Distribution of May Sales** in the title box. Then click Finish.

Excel 97. Complete the following four steps. Step 1—Your first decision is what type of chart you want. Line charts are recommended for showing behaviors over a time period, bar charts are good for comparing different items at the same point in time, and pie charts are used to show the relative proportion of elements that make up a whole. A pie chart is what you want in this tickler. Select the pie chart and pick the sub-type showing a 3-D Pie chart (middle option, top row). Then click Next. Step 2—Click Next. Step 3—For the title, enter **Distribution of May Sales** in the title box. Then click the Data Labels tab. Data Labels show certain kinds of data right on the face of the chart. Select the Data Labels to "Show percent," and click OK. Step 4—Click Finish.

6.   There are a number of ways to put your name on the chart. The three most convenient ways to do this are (1) add your name to the chart title, (2) use your name as an X-axis or Y-axis title, or (3) use a text box from the Drawing Toolbar. In Excel 97, you can also use WordArt from the Drawing Toolbar. Option 2 above cannot be used on a pie chart, but the other two options will be demonstrated here.

Select the title in the chart now. Then place the blinking insertion line right after the small "s" in Sales and press ENTER. This expands the title to a second line. Type in your name. You can put it in a smaller font if you want. Click elsewhere when done.

To use a text box, activate the Drawing Toolbar by clicking the Drawing button. Then click the Text Box button and draw a box somewhere on the chart. Type your name inside the box and use whatever formatting commands you feel are appropriate. Click elsewhere when done.

7.   Illustration SP-16 is how your chart might look. Save the file again as SAMPLE3 (use File Save).
8.   Select the chart and print it out using normal print commands.

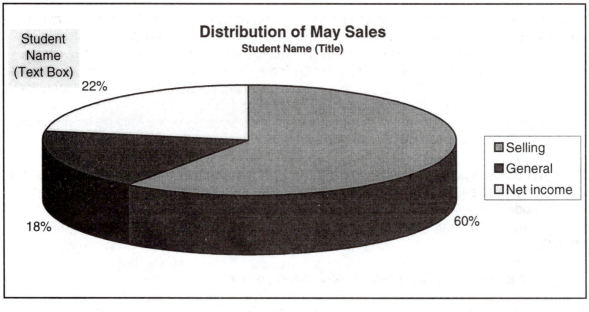

Illustration SP-16   *Completed Chart Tickler*

Sample Problem D

SAMPLE MODEL-BUILDING PROBLEM

Model-building problems require you to design spreadsheet models from start to finish. Nothing has been done for you. Completing the model-building problems will require a thorough knowledge of basic Excel skills. Lessons 1 through 5 of *Excel Quick*, a tutorial by Gaylord Smith specifically written for users of South-Western College Publishing's *Excel Spreadsheet Applications Series* should serve you well. In addition to the lessons, the tutorial provides three helpful appendices designed to assist in the model-building task. Appendix A covers built-in Excel functions useful for business models. Appendix B provides basic suggestions for developing spreadsheet models. Appendix C describes and shows several real world applications of Excel.

The model-building problems contain two sets of input plus an optional chart section. The first set of input is for you to use in designing your model. The second set will be used by your instructor to test your model to see if it performs the proper computations. Your instructor should not have to change anything in your model except the input data. Thus, you must be very careful in structuring your model.

You have been provided with both sets of data so that you can:

* specifically identify which variables in the problem will change and which ones won't
* double-check your model to see that it functions properly with different inputs

The purpose of this sample problem is to show you how to approach the model-building problems in this workbook. To accomplish this, you will work through the sample model-building problem that appears in Illustration SP-17. Read the problem now.

ORIGINAL DATA SOLUTION

Before turning on the computer, some attempt should be made to lay out the structure of your answer on paper. Careful planning on paper can eliminate hours of wasted time on the computer. Fortunately, spreadsheet programs are forgiving enough that most refinements to a preliminary plan can be done "on the fly" while working at the computer.

M# TRIAL BALANCE

The general ledger of Thistle Consulting shows the following account balances at May 31:

Cash	$ 8,217.10
Accounts receivable	94,062.28
Accounts payable	21,665.38
Chris McKeon, capital	80,614.00

Chris McKeon has asked you to develop a worksheet (file name BAL) that will present these numbers in a balance sheet format. Use the data above as input for your model.

Review the Model-Building Checklist on page 169 to ensure that your worksheet is complete. Print the file when done. *Check figure: Asset total, $102,279.38*

To test your model, use the following balances at June 30:

Cash	$31,484.20
Accounts receivable	65,415.51
Account payable	10,544.48
Chris McKeon, capital	86,355.23

Print the file again. *Check figure: Asset total, $96,899.71*

CHART (optional)

Prepare a chart that compares the individual asset balances at the end of May with the balances at the end of June. Print the chart when done.

Illustration SP-17   *Sample Model-Building Problem*

This model-building problem requires you to develop a spreadsheet model that is a balance sheet. Assuming you have had beginning accounting, you can probably visualize the answer format rather quickly. You might sketch out the following on paper to get you started.

Cash	$ 8,217.10	A/P	$21,665.38
A/R	94,062.28	Capital	80,614.00
	$ SUM		$ SUM

This is roughly what the answer will look like. The next major question to resolve is whether or not to use a Data Section for all of the changeable input values required to complete the model. A Data Section should always be given strong consideration since it helps highlight the numerical assumptions of the model, and it facilitates performing what-if analysis.

This decision relies on your judgment. As mentioned in Appendix B of *Excel Quick*, a direct-entry model is more appropriate than one using a Data Section in those cases where formulas do not have to be revised to accommodate the introduction of new data. In this balance sheet model, there are only two formulas (the sums at the bottom of each column), and they do not need to be rewritten as new data (account balances) are entered. Therefore, a direct-entry model is better for this particular model.

Now let's begin work on the computer. Start the spreadsheet program and, in the appropriate drive, insert the Student Disk or some other formatted disk.

You should enter your name and the file name somewhere at the top of the worksheet. As a suggestion, enter your name in cell A1. Enter the file name given to you in the problem in cell A2. The file name given for this problem is BAL. Do this now.

You will learn very quickly that making and correcting mistakes is a frequent occurrence when building models. Thus, in the instructions that follow, you will be purposely led into making a couple of mistakes and then shown how to correct them. Also, the Undo button can be very helpful for many types of errors. Turn to page 169 and review the Model-Building Checklist for some design suggestions.

Based on your initial plan, it appears that if you want the balance sheet somewhat centered on the screen, you can use columns B+C and F+G for entering account names and columns D and H for recording the balances. This will leave empty columns to the far left and far right of your page (columns A and I) for visual balance and an empty column down the middle (column E) to separate the two sides of the balance sheet. Let's start with this. You can always add new columns or eliminate extra columns later.

First, enter the basic data. Changes to formats, column widths, and so forth will be done later. Enter the following labels and values:

B7:	**Cash**
B8:	**Accounts receivable**
D7:	**8217.10**
D8:	**94062.28**
F7:	**Accounts payable**
F8:	**Chris McKeon, capital**
H7:	**21665.38**
H8:	**80614.00**

Move to cell D9, click the AutoSum button, and press ENTER. Do the same in cell H9. Your screen should appear as shown in Illustration SP-18.

	A	B	C	D	E	F	G	H
1	Student Name							
2	BAL							
3								
4								
5								
6								
7		Cash		8217.1		Accounts payable		21665.38
8		Accounts receivable		94062.28		Chris McKeon, capital		80614
9				102279.4				102279.4
10								

Illustration SP-18   *Sample Model-Building Worksheet—Stage 1*

In financial statements, dollar signs are usually placed at the top and bottom of columns. For this, the Currency or Accounting number formats are used. If you review Lesson 2 of *Excel Quick* you will be reminded that the Currency format places the dollar sign right next to the number (e.g., $8,217.10) and the Accounting format places the dollar sign to the left side of the cell (e.g., $ 8,217.10). Probably the best format when displaying a column of numbers is Accounting because the dollar signs at the top and bottom will automatically line up.

Move to cell D7, select the Cells command (Format menu), click the Number tab, and pick the Accounting category with two decimals and a dollar sign. (Excel 97 users, skip the rest of this paragraph.) Oops! You've got your first problem. In the Accounting format with two decimal places and a dollar sign, there are too many characters for the cell to hold. So, let's expand the width of column D. Place the mouse pointer on the line between the column headers D and E at the top of the worksheet. When positioned exactly on the line, the mouse pointer becomes a thick cross with arrowheads at both ends of the horizontal bar. Double-click the mouse button. This action automatically sets column D wide enough to see all the numbers in that column.

Next, move to cell D8 and put it in the Accounting format with two decimals and *no* dollar sign. Finally, move to cell D9 and put it in the Accounting format with two decimals and a dollar sign. You may need to widen column D to view the sum in cell D9.

Repeat these steps applying the Accounting format to the values in column H.

Now use the Borders button to place single underlines in cells D8 and H8, and double underlines in cells D9 and H9. See Illustration SP-19.

	A	B	C	D	E	F	G	H
1	Student Name							
2	BAL							
3								
4								
5								
6								
7		Cash		$ 8,217.10		Accounts payable		$ 21,665.38
8		Accounts receivable		94,062.28		Chris McKeon, capital		80,614.00
9				$ 102,279.38				$ 102,279.38
10								

Illustration SP-19   *Sample Model-Building Worksheet—Stage 2*

It now appears that if you widen columns B and F, you can get rid of columns C and G. It does no harm to leave the extra columns alone, but they are excess baggage. Let's first expand the width of column F. Place the mouse pointer on the line between the column headers F and G at the top of the worksheet. When positioned exactly on the line, the mouse pointer becomes a thick cross with arrowheads at both ends of the horizontal bar. Double-click the mouse button. This action automatically sets column F wide enough to see all the labels in that column. Next, to eliminate column G, click anywhere in column G, select the Delete command (Edit menu) and choose the Entire Column option.

Repeat this process to expand column B and eliminate column C.

Finally, use the mouse (or the Format Column Width command) to narrow the width of column D to about half of its current size. When done, your model should appear as in Illustration SP-20.

	A	B	C	D	E	F
1	Student Name					
2	BAL					
3						
4						
5						
6						
7		Cash	$ 8,217.10		Accounts payable	$ 21,665.38
8		Accounts receivable	94,062.28		Chris McKeon, capital	80,614.00
9			$ 102,279.38			$ 102,279.38
10						

Illustration SP-20   *Sample Model-Building Problem—Stage 3*

Looks pretty good! Now for some headings. It does not appear that there are enough empty rows at the top of the statement for these. Let's add three more rows. Select the range A4 to A6 and then choose the Insert Rows command. The first row of the statement is now pushed down to row 10.

The title for the statement will be most visually appealing if it is centered across the columns used in the worksheet. To accomplish this, enter the following labels:

B4:	**Thistle Consulting**
B5:	**Balance Sheet**
B6:	**As of May 31**

Next, select the range B4 to F4 (note: F4 not F6), click the Merge and Center button (in Excel 5.0 and Excel 95 it is the Center Across Columns button). This centers "Thistle Consulting" across columns B to F. Repeat this for the range B5 to F5 and then for B6 to F6. This will center each line of the heading above the statement.

Finally, select the range B4 to B6 and click the Bold button. This puts the title in bold print. Move to cell A1 and examine your masterpiece! Your worksheet should appear as shown in Illustration SP-21.

	A	B	C	D	E	F
1	Student Name					
2	BAL					
3						
4			**Thistle Consulting**			
5			**Balance Sheet**			
6			**As of May 31**			
7						
8						
9						
10		Cash	$ 8,217.10		Accounts payable	$ 21,665.38
11		Accounts receivable	94,062.28		Chris McKeon, capital	80,614.00
12			$ 102,279.38			$ 102,279.38
13						

Illustration SP-21   *Sample Model-Building Worksheet—Done!*

A quick review of the Model-Building Checklist on page 169 will indicate that you have followed most of its suggestions.

The last step is to protect your worksheet. Everything that will remain the same month after month should be protected. Items that will change should be left unprotected. Review the test data provided in the problem statement in Illustration SP-17. From this it is apparent that the account balances will (or could) change each month, as will the date.

To begin the protection process, select cell B6. Then, holding the CTRL key down, also select cells C10, C11, F10, and F11. Next, select the Cells command (Format menu), click the Protection tab, and click the Locked box to deselect it. Click OK. Finally, select the Protection command (Tools menu) and choose the Protect sheet option. Click OK.

Save the file as BAL (File Save As).

Print the file for submission to your instructor (File Print).

TEST DATA SOLUTION

Let's test your model now using the test data from Illustration SP-17. Move to cell B6, press the F2 (EDIT) key, press the BACKSPACE key several times to erase the May date, type **June 30**, and press ENTER. Next, enter all of the June 30 balances in the appropriate cells of the balance sheet. When done, your totals should balance, and they should agree with the check figure for June 30. *The check figure for the June asset total is $96,899.71.*

If you make any corrections to the original file, be sure to save the revised file again as BAL.

When the test data answer agrees with the check figure, the file can be printed again.

ORIGINAL SOLUTION WITH DATA SECTION

Before you leave this lesson, let's discuss what this model might have looked like if a Data Section had been used. Illustration SP-22 presents one possibility. The cells in the range C6 to C9 are unprotected as is cell B16 where the date is entered. Cells C20, C21, F20, and F21 in the Answer Section contain formulas which reference the appropriate cells in the Data Section. The formula in cell C20 is =C6, the formula in cell C21 is =C7, and so forth. This would be a good model design for a bookkeeper who had difficulty keeping assets, liabilities, and equity accounts straight!

	A	B	C	D	E	F
1	Student Name					
2	BAL					
3						
4	Data Section:					
5						
6		Cash	$ 21,665.30			
7		Accounts receivable	90,614.00			
8		Accounts payable	3,217.10			
9		Chris McKeon, capital	34,062.28			
10						
11	Answer Section:					
12						
13						
14			**Thistle Consulting**			
15			**Balance Sheet**			
16			**As of May 31**			
17						
18						
19						
20		Cash	$ 8,217.10		Accounts payable	$ 21,665.38
21		Accounts receivable	94,062.28		Chris McKeon, capital	80,614.00
22			$ 102,279.38			$ 102,279.38
23						

Illustration SP-22   *Sample Model-Building Worksheet with Data Section*

CHART SOLUTION (optional)

Open the file BAL now if it is not already on your screen. The optional chart section (see Illustration SP-17) calls for the creation of a chart based on data found in both months. The easiest way to handle this is to create a Chart Data Table first. The table should not interfere (physically or visually) with the worksheet itself. Let's place it beginning in row 22 using the following steps:

1. Select the Tools Protection command and unprotect the sheet.
2. Use the following table to enter the labels and values in the cells specified (the row and column labels are provided for reference only and should not be keyed). Do not be concerned with the date format Excel uses for your entries on row 23.

	A	B	C
22	**Chart Data**		
23		**May 31**	**June 30**
24	**Cash**	8217.1	31484.2
25	**Accts Rec**	94062.28	65415.51

28

3.   Select the range A23 to C25. Click the Chart Wizard button.

4.   **Excel 5.0 and Excel 95.** Now you need to position your new chart. Point to cell B26, hold down the mouse button and drag over an area down to cell F38. Release the mouse button. Then complete the following steps. Step 1—Click Next. Step 2—Line charts are recommended for showing behaviors over a time period, bar charts are good for comparing different items at the same point in time, and pie charts are used to show the relative proportion of elements that make up a whole. A column chart is what you want in this tickler. Pick the 3-D Column chart and click Next. Step 3—Pick sub-type #1. Click Next. Step 4—The current arrangement makes it somewhat difficult to compare May's cash balance with June's and the same for accounts receivable. Try the column orientation. Yes, that's better. Click Next. Step 5—Enter **Asset Balances** in the Chart Title box. You could enter a title for the Category (X) axis like "Accounts," but it is already pretty self-evident. Click Finish.

    Excel 97. Complete the following steps. Step 1—Your first decision is what type of chart you want. Line charts are recommended for showing behaviors over a time period, bar charts are good for comparing different items at the same point in time, and pie charts are used to show the relative proportion of elements that make up a whole. A column chart is what you want in this tickler. Select the column chart and pick the sub-type showing a 3-D Column chart (middle row, left side). Then click Next. Step 2—The current arrangement makes it somewhat difficult to compare May's cash balance with June's and the same for accounts receivable. Try the column orientation. Yes, that's better. Click Next. Step 3—For the Chart title, enter **Asset Balances** in the title box. You could enter a title for the Category (X) axis like "Accounts," but it is already pretty self-evident. Click Next. Step 4—Click Finish.

5.   In Excel 5.0 and Excel 95, double-click an open area of the chart to put it in the Edit mode (with dark border around it). In Excel 97, click the chart once to select it.

    Double-click the Value (Y) axis. Up pops the Format menu. Click the Number tab and choose the Currency format with no decimal places. Click OK. This places dollar signs on the values on the Y-axis.

6.   The dates in row 23 of the Chart Data Table are not really in the format you want. In fact there is no Excel format identical to what you initially entered in those cells. To force Excel to accept your original date entry format, you need to reenter the dates in row 23 placing an *apostrophe* in front of the dates. Do this now.

B23:   **'May 31**
C23:   **'June 30**

You may recall from Lesson 1 in *Excel Quick* that this is the way to force Excel to accept values and dates as labels. Your completed chart should appear now as shown in Illustration SP-23.

7.   Reprotect the file using the Tools Protection command.

8.   To print a chart, select it (click in an open area on the chart) and choose File Print. Or you can print the worksheet and the chart together by clicking the worksheet and choosing File Print. Do either of these now. Remember, color tends to muddy the printouts on a non-color printer.

9. A chart is saved when the file is saved. Select File Save As now and save the file as BAL, replacing the old version.

After your instructor has reviewed your work, you may erase the file BAL from your Student Disk to make room for future homework files.

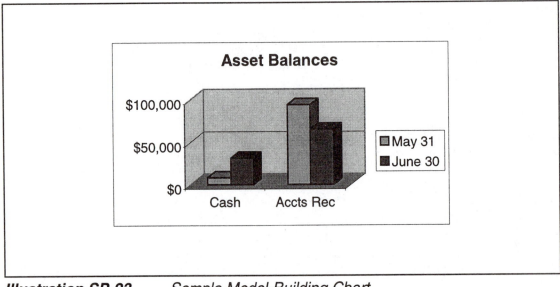

Illustration SP-23   *Sample Model-Building Chart*

P1 ☆ BUSINESS TRANSACTIONS (PTRANS)

LEARNING OBJECTIVES

- Show how financial position is affected by transactions.
- Prepare three basic proprietorship financial statements.
- Back-solve for cash balances.
- Alter the worksheet to accommodate additional transactions.
- Create a chart showing liability and equity categories.

PROBLEM DATA

On June 1 of the current year, Judy Meyers opened Meyers Professional Résumé Service. The sole proprietorship had the following transactions during June.

a. Opened a business checking account and made a deposit, $2,500.
b. Paid rent for June for office space and equipment, $500.
c. Purchased office supplies (stamps, pens, etc.) on account, $340.
d. Received cash for services rendered, $750.
e. Paid creditor for office supplies purchased on account, $250.
f. Purchased office supplies for cash, $95.
g. Billed clients for consultations performed on account, $1,100.
h. Paid utility bill of $90.
i. Paid the secretary's salary of $600.
j. Cash was withdrawn for owner's personal use, $250.
k. Received cash from clients previously billed, $750.
l. Returned $75 of office supplies purchased in transaction (f). Received a full refund.

REQUIRED

1. Review the printout of the worksheet PTRANS. You have been asked to complete the worksheet by recording these transactions.

2. There are five formulas requested to complete the worksheet. Using the spaces provided below, write the formulas required to complete the worksheet.

FORMULA1_____   FORMULA4_____

FORMULA2_____   FORMULA5_____

FORMULA3_____

3. Start the spreadsheet program and open the file PTRANS from the Student Disk. Enter the formulas in the appropriate cells on the worksheet. Then enter the increases and decreases resulting from each transaction on the worksheet. For example, the first transaction increases the cash account by $2,500 and also increases the capital account by $2,500. This transaction has already been recorded on the worksheet. The worksheet will automatically total each column as values are entered in that column. When you are finished, check line 26 to make sure that total assets equal total liabilities and equity.

4. It has been determined that the cost of the supplies used during the month was $150. Record the increase or decrease in the appropriate columns on the worksheet. This is transaction (m). Enter your name in cell A1. Save the completed file as PTRANS4. Print the worksheet. *Check figure: Ending cash balance (cell B21), $2,290.*

5. How does transaction (m) differ from transactions (a) through (l)? In other words, why is it treated as a special item?

6.   Use the space below to prepare an income statement, a statement of owner's equity, and a balance sheet in good form for Meyers Professional Résumé Service for the month of June.

WHAT-IF ANALYSIS

7. Judy initially invested $2,500 in the business. Could she have invested less? How little could she have invested initially and never have her cash balance go below zero? To help answer this question, move to column J and analyze the information provided. Then enter different amounts in cell B8 to help determine an answer. When you have determined an answer, use the File Print command to print the range A1 to J21 all on one page. Explain how you derived your answer below.

GRAPHICAL ANALYSIS

8. Reset cell B8 to $2,500. Click the Chart sheet tab. A pie chart appears on the screen indicating the percentage of each asset in relation to total assets. Judy does not want her cash balance to exceed 60% of her total assets. How much does she have to withdraw at month-end to reduce her cash percentage to 60%? To find out, enter different (negative) values in cell B20 of the worksheet and click the Chart sheet tab after each entry. When you find the withdrawal amount that decreases the cash percentage to 60%, enter that amount in the space provided below.

   Withdrawal needed $_____

   When the assignment is complete, close the file without saving it again.

TICKLERS (optional)

Worksheet. Two additional transactions occurred in June which need to be recorded on the worksheet.

n.   Billed customers for additional services rendered on account, $600.
o.   Paid creditor for office supplies purchased on account, $60.

Expand the PTRANS4 worksheet to include these transactions. Do not revise column J. Use the Print Preview command (File menu) to make sure that the worksheet will print neatly on one page, then print the worksheet. Save the revised file as PTRANST.

Chart. Using the PTRANS4 file, create a 3-D pie chart that shows the relative balances of the liability and equity accounts. Complete the Chart Tickler Data Table on the Chart worksheet and use it as a basis for preparing the chart. Put your name somewhere on the chart. Save the file again as PTRANS4. Select the chart and then print it out.

	A	B	C	D	E	F	G	H	I	J
2				*PTRANS*						
3				*Business Transactions*						
4										
5			Assets		=	Liabilities	+	Equity		Running
6			Accounts	Office		Accounts		Meyers,		Cash
7		Cash	Receivable	Supplies		Payable		Capital		Balance
8	a)	$2,500	$0	$0		$0		$2,500		$2,500
9	b)									2,500
10	c)									2,500
11	d)									2,500
12	e)									2,500
13	f)									2,500
14	g)									2,500
15	h)									2,500
16	i)									2,500
17	j)									2,500
18	k)									2,500
19	l)									2,500
20	m)									2,500
21		FORMULA1	FORMULA2	FORMULA3		FORMULA4		FORMULA5		
22										
23					Balance Verification					
24				Total assets				$0		
25				Total liabilities and equity				0		
26				Difference				$0		
27										

P2 ✫ WORKSHEET (P1WORK)

LEARNING OBJECTIVES

- Prepare a worksheet for a service firm.
- Prepare financial statements from a worksheet.
- Compare expense levels to national averages.
- Alter the worksheet to include a properly designed income statement.
- Create a chart showing the amount of all expenses.

PROBLEM DATA

The trial balance of Nikki Cleaners at December 31, 2000, the end of the current fiscal year, is below:

Nikki Cleaners
Trial Balance
December 31, 2000

Cash	$ 6,600	
Cleaning Supplies	11,000	
Prepaid Insurance	2,700	
Equipment	103,000	
Accumulated Depreciation		$ 37,050
Accounts Payable		3,720
Nikki Lee, Capital		67,800
Nikki Lee, Drawing	27,000	
Revenue		77,610
Rent Expense	14,250	
Wages Expense	19,860	
Utilities Expense	1,065	
Miscellaneous Expense	705	
	$186,180	$186,180

Information for the adjusting entries is as follows:

a. Cleaning supplies on hand on December 31, 2000, $9,375.
b. Insurance premiums expired during the year, $900.
c. Depreciation on equipment during the year, $10,800.
d. Wages accrued but not paid at December 31, 2000, $915.

REQUIRED

1. As the accountant for Nikki Cleaners, you have been asked to prepare financial statements for the year. A file called P1WORK has been provided to assist you in this assignment. As you review this file, it should be noted that columns H and I will automatically change when you enter values in columns E or G.

2. There are eight formulas requested to complete the file. Using the spaces provided below, write the formulas required to complete the file.

    FORMULA1_____   FORMULA5_____

    FORMULA2_____   FORMULA6_____

    FORMULA3_____   FORMULA7_____

    FORMULA4_____   FORMULA8_____

3. Start the spreadsheet program and open the file P1WORK from the Student Disk. Enter the formulas in the appropriate cells on the worksheet. Then enter the adjusting amounts in columns E and G. Also, in column D or F, insert the letter corresponding to the adjusting entry (a–d). Column A is "frozen" on the screen to assist you in completing requirement 4.

4. Complete the income statement and balance sheet columns by entering formulas in columns J, K, L, and M that reference the appropriate cells in columns H or I. Net income will be automatically calculated for the income statement and balance sheet. Check to be sure that these numbers are the same. Enter your name in cell A1. Save the completed file as P1WORK4. Print the worksheet. *Check figure: Net income (cell J29), $27,490.*

WHAT-IF ANALYSIS

5. Suppose you discover that an assistant in your department had misunderstood your instructions and had provided you with wrong information on two of the adjusting entries. Cleaning supplies consumed during the year should have been $9,375, and insurance premiums unexpired at year-end were $900. Make the corrections on your worksheet and save the corrected file as P1WORK5. Reprint the worksheet.

6. Use the space below to prepare an income statement, a capital statement, and a balance sheet, using the corrected worksheet (P1WORK5). Assume that no additional owner investments were made during the year.

GRAPHICAL ANALYSIS

7.   With the P1WORK5 file open, click the Chart sheet tab. On the screen, a pie chart shows the percentage composition of the total expenses of Nikki Cleaners. Enter the percentages below. Compare the percentages of Nikki Cleaners with the national statistics provided.

	National Averages	**Nikki Cleaners**
Rent	12.3%	_____
Utilities	7.7	_____
Wages	33.0	_____
Miscellaneous	1.0	_____
Supplies	17.5	_____
Insurance	4.7	_____
Depreciation	23.8	_____
	100.0%	100.0%

Comment on the differences noted. Why might depreciation, utilities, and rent be so far off from the national percentages? When the assignment is complete, close the file without saving it again.

TICKLERS (optional)

Worksheet. You prepared an income statement in requirement 6. Put a formal income statement somewhere on the P1WORK5 worksheet. Enter formulas in the income statement to reference the appropriate income statement cells in the worksheet. Use proper formats for all value cells. Put your name above the income statement. Print your work (select and print just the income statement cells). Use the Print Preview command (File menu) to make sure that the income statement alone (not the whole worksheet) will print neatly on one page. Save the completed file as P1WORKT.

Chart. Using the P1WORK5 file, create a 3-D column chart showing the dollar total of each of the expenses of Nikki Cleaners. Use the Chart Data Table as a basis for preparing the chart. Use appropriate titles, legends, and formats. Put your name somewhere on the chart. Save the file again as P1WORK5. Select the chart and then print it out.

Nikki Cleaners
Work Sheet
For Year Ended December 31, 2000

Account Title	Trial Balance Dr.	Trial Balance Cr.	Adjustments Dr.	Adjustments Cr.	Adj. T/Balance Dr.	Adj. T/Balance Cr.	Income Statement Dr.	Income Statement Cr.	Balance Sheet Dr.	Balance Sheet Cr.
Cash	6,600				6,600	0				
Cleaning supplies	11,000				11,000	0				
Prepaid insurance	2,700				2,700	0				
Equipment	103,000				103,000	0				
Accumulated depr.		37,050			0	37,050				
Accounts payable		3,720			0	3,720				
Nikki Lee, capital		67,800			0	67,800				
Nikki Lee, drawing	27,000				27,000	0				
Revenue		77,610			0	77,610				
Rent expense	14,250				14,250	0				
Wages expense	19,860				19,860	0				
Utilities expense	1,065				1,065	0				
Misc. expense	705				705	0				
	186,180	186,180								
Supplies expense					0	0				
Insurance expense					0	0				
Depreciation exp.					0	0				
Wages payable					0	0				
Net income							0	0	0	0
							0	0	0	0

FORM1 FORM2 FORM3 FORM4 FORM5 FORM6 FORM7 FORM8

41

P3 ☼ MERCHANDISING WORKSHEET (P2WORK)

LEARNING OBJECTIVES

- Prepare a worksheet for a merchandising firm.
- Prepare financial statements from a worksheet.
- Compare expense levels to national averages.
- Alter the worksheet to include a properly designed balance sheet.
- Create a chart showing all expenses.

PROBLEM DATA

The trial balance of Comtronics at June 30, 2000, the end of the current fiscal year, is as follows:

Comtronics
Trial Balance
June 30, 2000

Cash	$ 6,069	
Accounts Receivable	13,890	
Merchandise Inventory	23,982	
Prepaid Insurance	2,205	
Store Supplies	1,185	
Store Equipment	15,000	
Accumulated Depreciation		$ 1,500
Accounts Payable		6,210
L. Wilson, Capital		41,280
L. Wilson, Drawing	7,200	
Sales		149,700
Purchases	96,450	
Advertising Expense	3,975	
Rent Expense	6,000	
Salaries Expense	19,920	
Utilities Expense	2,814	
	$198,690	$198,690

Adjustment information is as follows:

a. Supplies on hand as of June 30, 2000, $225.
b. Insurance premiums that expired during the year, $1,210.
c. Depreciation on equipment during the year, $750.
d. Salaries accrued but not paid at June 30, 2000, $720.
e. Merchandise inventory on June 30, 2000, $21,932.

43

REQUIRED

1. As the accountant for Comtronics, you have been asked to prepare adjusting entries, financial statements, and closing entries to complete the accounting cycle for the year. A worksheet called P2WORK has been provided to assist you in this assignment. As you review this worksheet, it should be noted that columns H and I will automatically change when you enter values in columns E and G.

2. There are eight formulas requested to complete the worksheet. Using the spaces provided below, write the formulas required to complete the worksheet.

   FORMULA1_____   FORMULA5_____

   FORMULA2_____   FORMULA6_____

   FORMULA3_____   FORMULA7_____

   FORMULA4_____   FORMULA8_____

3. Start the spreadsheet program and open the file P2WORK from the Student Disk. Enter the formulas in the appropriate cells on the worksheet. Then enter the adjusting amounts in columns E and G. Also, in column D or F insert the letter corresponding to the adjusting entry (a—e). (*Note:* Not all textbooks handle the change in inventory as an adjustment. Use the method for handling inventory that is prescribed in your textbook.) Column A is "frozen" on the screen to assist you in completing requirement 4 below.

4. Complete the income statement and balance sheet by entering formulas in columns J, K, L, and M that reference the appropriate cells in column H or I. Net income will be automatically calculated at the bottom of the income statement and balance sheet columns. Check to be sure that these numbers are the same. Enter your name in cell A1. Save the completed file as P2WORK4. Print the worksheet. *Check figure: Net income (cell J33), $14,851.*

WHAT-IF ANALYSIS

5. You discover that your boss has mistakenly provided you with wrong information on two of the adjusting entries. Expired insurance premiums should have been $1,710, and unpaid salaries should have been $1,220. Make the corrections on your worksheet and save the corrected file as P2WORK5. Reprint the worksheet.

6.   In the space provided below, prepare an income statement, a capital statement (statement of owner's equity), and a balance sheet. Use the corrected worksheet (P2WORK5) as a basis for your work. Assume no additional owner investments were made during the year.

GRAPHICAL ANALYSIS

7. Open P2WORK5 and click the Chart sheet tab. On the screen, a pie chart shows the percentage composition of the total expenses of Comtronics. Enter the percentages below.

	National Averages	Comtronics
Cost of goods sold	65.0%	_____
Salaries	20.0	_____
Utilities	4.0	_____
Depreciation	4.0	_____
Insurance	3.0	_____
Supplies	2.0	_____
Rent	1.0	_____
Advertising	1.0	_____
	100.0%	100.0%

Compare the percentages of Comtronics with the national statistics provided. Comment on the differences noted. Why might depreciation, utilities, and rent (as a group) be so far off from the national percentages? Any explanation for salaries? COGS? When the assignment is complete, close the file without saving it again.

TICKLERS (optional)

Worksheet. You prepared a balance sheet in requirement 6. Put a formal balance sheet somewhere on the P2WORK5 worksheet. Enter formulas in the balance sheet to reference the appropriate balance sheet cells in the worksheet. Use proper formats for all value cells. Put your name above the balance sheet. Print your work (select and print just the balance sheet cells). Use the Print Preview command (File menu) to make sure that the balance sheet alone (not the whole worksheet) will print neatly on one page. Save the completed file as P2WORKT.

P2WORK
Merchandising Worksheet

Comtronics
Work Sheet
For Year Ended June 30, 2000

Account Title	Trial Balance Dr.	Trial Balance Cr.	Adjustments Dr.	Adjustments Cr.	Adj. T/Balance Dr.	Adj. T/Balance Cr.	Income Statement Dr.	Income Statement Cr.	Balance Sheet Dr.	Balance Sheet Cr.
Cash	6,069				6,069	0				
Accts receivable	13,890				13,890	0				
Merchandise inv.	23,982				23,982	0				
Prepaid insurance	2,205				2,205	0				
Store Supplies	1,185				1,185	0				
Store equipment	15,000				15,000	0				
Accum. deprec.		1,500			0	1,500				
Accounts payable		6,210			0	6,210				
L. Wilson, capital		41,280			0	41,280				
L. Wilson, drawing	7,200				7,200	0				
Sales		149,700			0	149,700				
Purchases	96,450				96,450	0				
Advertising exp.	3,975				3,975	0				
Rent expense	6,000				6,000	0				
Salaries exp.	19,920				19,920	0				
Utilities exp.	2,814				2,814	0				
	198,690	198,690								
Income summary					0	0				
Supplies expense					0	0				
Insurance expense					0	0				
Depreciation exp.					0	0				
Salaries payable					0	0				
	FORM1	FORM2	FORM3	FORM4			FORM5	FORM6	FORM7	FORM8
Net income							0	0	0	0
							0	0	0	0

P4 ☼ MERCHANDISING ENTERPRISE (PMERCH)

LEARNING OBJECTIVES

- Prepare financial statements for a merchandising firm.
- Compare and analyze the change in balances over two months.
- Analyze five-month trends in sales, gross profit, and net income.
- Alter the worksheet by rearranging the order of the Answer Section.
- Create a chart showing the amount of all selling expenses.

PROBLEM DATA

The following information is for Continental Industries for the month ended April 30, 2000:

Accounts Payable	$207,000	Prepaid Insurance	$ 24,000
Accounts Receivable	222,915	Purchases	419,000
Accum. Depreciation—		Purchases Discount	54,325
Store Equipment	304,500	Rent Expense—General	4,500
Advertising Expense	33,000	Rent Expense—Selling	15,000
Baker, Capital, beginning	270,000	Salaries Expense—General	18,000
Baker, Drawing	144,000	Salaries Expense—Selling	96,000
Cash	53,580	Salaries Payable	12,300
Depreciation Expense	9,000	Sales	760,000
Insurance Expense—General	900	Sales Discount	48,000
Insurance Expense—Selling	8,100	Store Equipment	375,000
Merchandise Inventory, beginning	117,000	Store Supplies	5,880
Merchandise Inventory, ending	155,000	Store Supplies Expense	14,250

REQUIRED

1. Review the worksheet called PMERCH that follows these requirements. You have been asked to prepare Continental's financial statements using this worksheet. Note that the data from the problem have already been entered into the top section of the worksheet. Cells that contain zeros on the worksheet already have formulas entered in them. As you enter formulas onto the worksheet, these zeros will be replaced by values.

2. Using the spaces provided below, write the formulas and titles where requested in the worksheet. FORMULA2 and TITLE A have been written for you as examples.

FORMULA1	_____	FORMULA17	_____
FORMULA2	_____ **=G28** _____	FORMULA18	_____
FORMULA3	_____	FORMULA19	_____
FORMULA4	_____	FORMULA20	_____
FORMULA5	_____	FORMULA21	_____
FORMULA6	_____	FORMULA22	_____
FORMULA7	_____	FORMULA23	_____
FORMULA8	_____	FORMULA24	_____
FORMULA9	_____	FORMULA25	_____
FORMULA10	_____	FORMULA26	_____
FORMULA11	_____	FORMULA27	_____
FORMULA12	_____	FORMULA28	_____
FORMULA13	_____	FORMULA29	_____
FORMULA14	_____	FORMULA30	_____
FORMULA15	_____	FORMULA31	_____
FORMULA16	_____	FORMULA32	_____
TITLE A	_____ **Sales Discount** _____	TITLE I	_____
TITLE B	_____	TITLE J	_____
TITLE C	_____	TITLE K	_____
TITLE D	_____	TITLE L	_____
TITLE E	_____	TITLE M	_____
TITLE F	_____	TITLE N	_____
TITLE G	_____	TITLE O	_____

TITLE Q_____   TITLE U_____

TITLE R_____   TITLE V_____

TITLE S_____   TITLE W_____

TITLE T_____   TITLE X_____

3.   Start the spreadsheet program and open the file PMERCH from the Student Disk. Enter all formulas and titles where indicated on the worksheet. When you are finished, make sure that your balance sheet balances. Enter your name in cell A1. Save your completed file as PMERCH3. Print the worksheet. *Check figure: Total assets (cell G109), $531,875.*

WHAT-IF ANALYSIS

4.   To test your model, enter the following data in the Data Section for the month ended May 31, 2000.

Accounts Payable	$157,500	Prepaid Insurance	$ 14,175
Accounts Receivable	199,200	Purchases	400,500
Accum. Depreciation—		Purchases Discount	30,000
Store Equipment	316,500	Rent Expense—General	4,500
Advertising Expense	72,000	Rent Expense—Selling	15,000
Baker, Capital, beginning	312,575	Salaries Expense—General	27,000
Baker, Drawing	127,000	Salaries Expense—Selling	120,000
Cash	37,765	Salaries Payable	6,900
Depreciation Expense	12,000	Sales	862,500
Insurance Expense—General	975	Sales Discount	37,500
Insurance Expense—Selling	8,850	Store Equipment	435,000
Merchandise Inventory, beginning	154,500	Store Supplies	3,360
Merchandise Inventory, ending	93,000	Store Supplies Expense	16,650

When you are finished, make sure your balance sheet balances. Save your completed file as PMERCH4. Reprint the worksheet.

5.   Compare the April and May income statements. Comment on any trends noted.

GRAPHICAL ANALYSIS

6. Click the Chart sheet tab on the PMERCH4 file. You will see a chart depicting the five-month trend in sales, gross profit, and net income. What favorable and unfavorable trends do you see in this month-to-month comparison? Comment on any unusual changes.

When the assignment is complete, close the file without saving it again.

TICKLERS (optional)

Worksheet. Your boss would prefer to have the balance sheet shown before the income statement and the capital statement. Please make this change on the PMERCH4 file. Use the Print Preview command (File menu) to make sure that the worksheet will print neatly on two or three pages, then print the worksheet. Save the completed file as PMERCHT.

Chart. Using the PMERCH4 file, prepare a 3-D pie chart that shows the amount of each of the selling expenses in May. No Chart Data Table is needed. Select A56 to A61 as one range on the worksheet to be charted and then hold down the CTRL key and select E56 to E61 as the second range. Put your name somewhere on the chart. Save the file again as PMERCH4. Select the chart and then print it out.

	A	B	C	D	E	F	G
2				PMERCH			
3				Merchandising Enterprise			
4							
5	Data Section					Month:	April 30, 2000
6							
7	Accounts Payable						$207,000
8	Accounts Receivable						222,915
9	Accumulated Depreciation-Store Equipment						304,500
10	Advertising Expense						33,000
11	Baker, Capital - beginning						270,000
12	Baker, Drawing						144,000
13	Cash						53,580
14	Depreciation Expense-Store Equipment						9,000
15	Insurance Expense-General						900
16	Insurance Expense-Selling						8,100
17	Merchandise Inventory, beginning						117,000
18	Merchandise Inventory, ending						155,000
19	Prepaid Insurance						24,000
20	Purchases						419,000
21	Purchases Discount						54,325
22	Rent Expense-General						4,500
23	Rent Expense-Selling						15,000
24	Salaries Expense-General						18,000
25	Salaries Expense-Selling						96,000
26	Salaries Payable						12,300
27	Sales						760,000
28	Sales Discount						48,000
29	Store Equipment						375,000
30	Store Supplies						5,880
31	Store Supplies Expense						14,250

	A	B	C	D	E	F	G
33	Answer Section						
34							
35				Continental Industries			
36				Income Statement			
37				For Month Ended			
38				April 30, 2000			
39							
40	Revenue:						
41	Sales					FORMULA1	
42	Less:	TITLE A				FORMULA2	
43	Net sales						FORMULA3
44	Cost of goods sold:						
45	Beginning merchandise inventory					$0	
46	TITLE B				FORMULA4		
47	Less:	TITLE C			FORMULA5		
48	Net purchases					FORMULA6	
49	Goods available for sale					$0	
50	Less ending inventory					FORMULA7	
51	Cost of goods sold						FORMULA8
52	TITLE D						$0
53							
54	Operating expenses:						
55	Selling expenses:						
56	TITLE E				FORMULA9		
57	TITLE F				FORMULA10		
58	TITLE G				FORMULA11		
59	TITLE H				FORMULA12		
60	TITLE I				FORMULA13		
61	TITLE J				FORMULA14		
62	Total selling expenses					$0	
63	General expenses:						
64	TITLE K				FORMULA15		
65	TITLE L				FORMULA16		
66	TITLE M				FORMULA17		
67	Total general expenses					0	
68	Total operating expenses						0
69	Net income						FORMULA18
70							

	A	B	C	D	E	F	G
72					Continental Industries		
73					Capital Statement		
74					For Month Ended		
75					April 30, 2000		
76							
77	Beginning balance, capital						FORMULA19
78	Net income					FORMULA20	
79	TITLE N					FORMULA21	
80	Change in capital						FORMULA22
81	Ending balance, capital						$0
82							
83							
84					Continental Industries		
85					Balance Sheet		
86					April 30, 2000		
87							
88					Assets		
89	Current assets:						
90	TITLE O					FORMULA23	
91	TITLE P					FORMULA24	
92	TITLE Q					FORMULA25	
93	TITLE R					FORMULA26	
94	TITLE S					FORMULA27	
95	Total current assets						$0
96	Fixed assets:						
97	TITLE T					FORMULA28	
98	TITLE U					FORMULA29	
99	Total fixed assets						0
100	Total assets						$0
101							
102					Liabilities & Capital		
103	Liabilities:						
104	TITLE V					FORMULA30	
105	TITLE W					FORMULA31	
106	Total liabilities						$0
107	Capital:						
108	TITLE X						FORMULA32
109	Total liabilities & capital						$0
110							

P5 ✿ PURCHASES JOURNAL (PJOURNAL)

LEARNING OBJECTIVES

* Use a special purpose journal for credit purchases.
* Explain the use of an accounts payable subsidiary ledger.
* Interpret various levels of purchases.
* Alter the file by including new categories of purchases.
* Create a chart showing purchases of merchandise and supplies.

PROBLEM DATA

During the month of June, Bluebird Industries completed the following purchases on account and the related returns and allowances:

June
  1 Purchased merchandise on account from Team One, $6,390.
  3 Purchased store supplies on account from Wilson Supply Co., $1,325.
  4 Purchased merchandise on account from Bearmans Inc., $4,011.
  5 Purchased office equipment on account from EXP Equipment, $2,550.
  10 Received a credit memorandum from Team One for merchandise returned, $765.
  11 Purchased store supplies on account from Print 'n Press, $714.
  15 Received a credit memorandum on account from Bearmans Inc. as an allowance for damaged merchandise, $329.
  17 Purchased merchandise on account from Pro Distributors, $10,815.
  19 Purchased merchandise on account from Bearmans Inc., $2,800.
  21 Received a credit memorandum from Print 'n Press for store supplies returned, $108.
  22 Purchased store supplies on account from Wilson Supply Co., $1,080.

REQUIRED

1. You have been asked to record these transactions using a purchases journal and a general journal. The file called PJOURNAL is a computerized purchases journal. Since purchases journals vary in format, review the PJOURNAL file now. Bluebird Industries uses its purchases journal to record all acquisitions made on account including inventory, supplies, and equipment. Returns and allowances are recorded in the general journal. Note that formulas are required for the totals.

2. In the spaces provided below, enter the six formulas required.

    FORMULA1_____   FORMULA4_____

    FORMULA2_____   FORMULA5_____

    FORMULA3_____   FORMULA6_____

    In the spaces provided below, indicate whether the titles in row 8 should be Dr. or Cr.

    TITLE A_____   TITLE C_____

    TITLE B_____

3. Start the spreadsheet program and open the file PJOURNAL from the Student Disk. Enter the titles and formulas in the appropriate cells on the worksheet. Then record the purchase transactions on the computer in PJOURNAL and record other activities as general journal entries in the space provided below. Use general journal entries only for transactions not entered in the purchases journal. The first transaction in the purchases journal has been recorded for you. When you are finished, enter your name in cell A1. Save the file as PJJUN. Print the worksheet. *Check figure: Total credits to accounts payable (cell C20), $29,685.*

4. Assume that Bluebird Industries uses an accounts payable subsidiary ledger. In the space provided below, describe to a colleague how the journal is to be posted. Provide details.

WHAT-IF ANALYSIS

5.   Erase the transactions recorded in PJJUN and record the following transactions that occurred in July:

July
1	Purchased store supplies on account from Print 'n Press, $205.
5	Purchased merchandise on account from Bearmans Inc., $5,730.
7	Purchased merchandise on account from Turf Products, $13,800.
13	Purchased store equipment on account from Montano's, $900.
22	Purchased merchandise on account from Bearmans Inc., $3,300.
27	Purchased store supplies on account from Wilson Supply Co., $1,680.

Save the results as PJJUL. Print the worksheet.

GRAPHICAL ANALYSIS

6.   Janice Bluebird, the owner of Bluebird Industries, has been advised that as a rule of thumb she should keep her supplies purchases to less than 10% of her total supplies and merchandise purchases. Open the PJJUN file and click the Chart sheet tab. Is the goal met in June? Explain. Open the PJJUL file and click the Chart sheet tab. Is the goal met in July? Explain.

When the assignment is complete, close the files without saving them again.

TICKLERS (optional)

Worksheet. At the present time, Bluebird Industries only sells softball equipment. However, the owner has decided to expand the business by also selling golf equipment. Modify the PJJUN worksheet to include two categories of purchases. Use the current column for softball purchases and add a new column for golf purchases. Then record the entry for the following transaction:

June 29   Purchased merchandise on account from Bearmans Inc.: softball equipment, $1,350; golf equipment, $3,000.

Use the Print Preview command (File menu) to make sure that the worksheet will print neatly on one page, then print the worksheet. Save the completed file as PJJUNT.

Chart. Using the PJJUN file, create a 3-D column chart showing the dollars of merchandise purchases and supplies purchases. Use the Chart Data Table as a basis for preparing the chart. Put your name somewhere on the chart. Save the file again as PJJUN. Select the chart and then print it out.

	A	B	C	D	E	F	G
2				*PJOURNAL*			
3				*Purchases Journal*			
4							
5				Purchases Journal			Page 17
6			Accounts		Store	Sundry Accounts Dr.	
7			Payable	Purchases	Supplies	Account	
8	Date	Account Credited	TITLEA	TITLEB	TITLEC	Name	Amount
9	June						
10	1	Team One	6,390	6,390			
11							
12							
13							
14							
15							
16							
17							
18							
19							
20	Totals		FORMU1	FORMU2	FORMU3		FORMU4
21							
22						Balance Verification	
23						Total debits	FORMU5
24						Total credits	FORMU6
25						Difference	0
26							
27							

60

P6 ☼ BANK RECONCILIATION (BANKREC)

LEARNING OBJECTIVES

- Prepare a bank reconciliation and the necessary adjusting journal entries.
- Prepare a bank reconciliation with incomplete data.
- Interpret differences between book and bank balances.
- Alter the file to accept additional outstanding checks.
- Create a chart plotting book and bank balances.

PROBLEM DATA

Young's Drug Store deposits all receipts in a night depository after banking hours. The data needed to reconcile the bank statement as of September 30, 2000, have been extracted from records and are as follows:

From Young's records:

Checking account balance as of August 31	$8,720.23
Cash received and deposited in September (detail below*)	4,735.45
Checks written during September (detail below**)	- 4,828.88
Checkbook balance as of September 30	$8,626.80

*   Date and amount of each deposit in September: Sept. 3, $545.25; Sept. 8, $842.00; Sept. 11, $978.35; Sept. 16, $658.05; Sept. 19, $643.90; Sept. 24, $352.62; Sept. 28, $715.28.

**   Number and amount of each check issued in September:

No.	Amount	No.	Amount	No.	Amount	No.	Amount
750	$361.90	754	$869.52	758	$246.60	762	$236.74
751	64.71	755	471.86	759	Void	763	Void
752	462.18	756	156.20	760	87.95	764	210.00
753	51.90	757	274.35	761	719.27	765	615.70

From September's bank statement:

Balance as of August 31	$ 9,568.63
Deposits recorded in September (detail below*)	4,382.07
Checks charged to account in September (detail below**)	- 4,180.93
Other adjustments (detail below***)	1,387.80
Balance as of September 30	$11,157.57

*   Date and amount of each deposit in September: Sept. 1, $361.90; Sept. 4, $545.25; Sept. 9, $842.00; Sept. 12, $978.35; Sept. 17, $658.05; Sept. 20, $643.90; Sept. 25, $352.62.

**   Number and amount of each check in September:

No.	Amount	No.	Amount	No.	Amount	No.	Amount
740	$ 90.60	751	$ 64.71	755	$471.86	758	$264.60
747	217.45	752	462.18	756	156.20	760	87.95
748	570.97	753	51.90	757	274.35	762	236.74
750	361.90	754	869.52				

***   Description of each memo accompanying September's bank statement:

Date	Description	Amount
Sept. 4	Bank debit memo for check returned because of insufficient funds	$ 64.20
Sept. 12	Bank credit memo for note collected:	
	Principal	1,400.00
	Interest	60.00
Sept. 30	Bank debit memo for service charges	8.00

REQUIRED

1.   As treasurer, you have been asked to prepare a bank reconciliation as of September 30. Review the file called BANKREC that follows these requirements. The bank reconciliation as of August 31 is provided for you as a sample completed worksheet. You may need to refer to the August 31 bank reconciliation for information on outstanding checks.

2.   Using the spaces provided below, write the formulas where requested in the file. Carefully review the August 31 printout and note that subtractions are entered as negative numbers.

       FORMULA1_____   FORMULA3_____

       FORMULA2_____

3.   Start the spreadsheet program and open the file BANKREC from the Student Disk. Enter the formulas where indicated on the worksheet. Prepare a bank reconciliation as of September 30. Assume that all errors are the depositor's fault. Checks 754–757 were for salaries; all other checks were payments to suppliers on account. The reconciliation is not complete until the difference between the adjusted balances (cell C45) is zero. Enter your name in cell A1. Save your completed file as SEP30. Print the worksheet. *Check figure: Adjusted balance (cell E25), $9,996.60.*

4.   In the space provided below, prepare the necessary adjusting journal entries.

WHAT-IF ANALYSIS

5.   Erase all September data and use the worksheet to complete the following bank reconciliation at October 31, 2000:

Adjusted balance	$7,608
Balance per bank	7,950
Balance per books	?
Checks outstanding	547
Deposits in transit	?
Service charges	16

Save your completed file as OCT31. Print the worksheet.

GRAPHICAL ANALYSIS

6.   Open the SEP30 file. Click the Chart sheet tab. On the screen, a column chart appears illustrating relative book and bank balances at June 30 and July 31. In the space provided below, list at least two reasons why the discrepancy between book and bank balances may have existed at June 30.

a.

b.

Why may it have existed at July 31?

a.

b.

When the assignment is complete, close the file without saving it again.

TICKLERS (optional)

Worksheet. Suppose that there are ten checks outstanding at the end of December 2000. Modify the BANKREC worksheet to accept additional outstanding checks. Put your name in cell A1. Use the Print Preview command (File menu) to make sure that the worksheet will print neatly on one page, then print the worksheet. Save the completed file as BANKRECT.

Chart. Using the SEP30 file, prepare a line chart to show both the monthly ending bank balance and the adjusted book balance from June 30 through October 31. Use the Chart Data Table as a basis for preparing the chart. Expand the table to include data for August, September, and October based on the information provided in the problem. Put your name somewhere on the chart. Save the file again as BANKREC5. Select the chart and then print it out.

	A	B	C
2		**BANKREC**	
3		*Bank Reconciliation*	
4			
5		Young's Drug Store	
6		Bank Reconciliation	
7		September 30, 19X9	
8			
9			
10	Balance per bank statement		$0.00
11			
12	Additions by depositor not on bank statement:		
13			
14			
15			
16	Deductions by depositor not on bank statement:		
17			
18			
19			
20			
21			
22			
23	Bank errors:		
24			
25	Adjusted balance		FORMULA1
26			
27			
28	Balance per books		$0.00
29			
30	Additions by bank not recorded by depositor:		
31			
32			
33			
34	Deductions by bank not recorded by depositor:		
35			
36			
37			
38			
39			
40	Depositor's errors:		
41			
42	Adjusted balance		FORMULA2
43			
44			
45	Difference between adjusted balances		FORMULA3
46			

	A	B	C
2		**BANKREC**	
3		*Bank Reconciliation*	
4			
5		Young's Drug Store	
6		Bank Reconciliation	
7		August 31, 19X9	
8			
9			
10	Balance per bank statement		$9,568.63
11			
12	Additions by depositor not on bank statement:		
13		Deposit in transit 8/31	361.90
14			
15			
16	Deductions by depositor not on bank statement:		
17		Checks outstanding	
18		740	(90.60)
19		747	(217.45)
20		748	(570.97)
21		749	(331.28)
22			
23	Bank errors:		
24			
25	Adjusted balance		$8,720.23
26			
27			
28	Balance per books		$8,728.23
29			
30	Additions by bank not recorded by depositor:		
31			
32			
33			
34	Deductions by bank not recorded by depositor:		
35		Service charge	(8.00)
36			
37			
38			
39			
40	Depositor's errors:		
41			
42	Adjusted balance		$8,720.23
43			
44			
45	Difference between adjusted balances		$0.00
46			
47			

P7 ☼ AGING ACCOUNTS RECEIVABLE (AGING)

LEARNING OBJECTIVES

- Prepare an accounts receivable aging schedule.
- Apply the allowance method of accounting for uncollectible accounts.
- Interpret changes in collection patterns.
- Alter the file to include one additional customer.
- Create a chart showing estimated uncollectible balances by age category.

PROBLEM DATA

On October 31, 2000, Turbo Transformers Inc., an on-site business systems consulting firm, had the following amounts due from its customers:

Customer	Total	Not Yet Due	1–30 Days Past Due	31–60 Days Past Due	61–90 Days Past Due	Over 90 Days Past Due
A. J. Point	$ 1,800	$1,300	$ 350			$150
G. Shrub	3,750	2,800	950			
ITT Tech	5,000	1,500	1,500	$1,000	$1,000	
Oxford Inc.	1,900	1,900				
Silver Screen	400				400	
Stock & Well	1,750		500	320	700	230
Totals	$14,600	$7,500	$ 3,300	$1,320	$1,700	$780

Based on the company's past experience, it has established the following percentages for estimating uncollectible accounts:

Age Interval	Percent Uncollectible
Not yet due	1%
1–30 days past due	3
31–60 days past due	5
61–90 days past due	10
Over 90 days past due	25

REQUIRED

1. You have been asked to estimate the total amount of uncollectible accounts expense as of October 31 by completing the file called AGING.

2. Using the spaces provided below, write the formulas where requested in the file. FORMULA1 has been done for you as an example.

    FORMULA1 _____=D21_____   FORMULA7_____

    FORMULA2_____   FORMULA8_____

    FORMULA3_____   FORMULA9_____

    FORMULA4_____   FORMULA10_____

    FORMULA5_____   FORMULA11_____

    FORMULA6_____   FORMULA12_____

3. Start the spreadsheet program and open the file AGING from the Student Disk. Enter all formulas where indicated on the worksheet. Enter your name in cell A1. Save your completed file as AGING3. Print the worksheet. *Check figure: Total uncollectible (cell F28), $605.*

4. Assume that October's credit sales were $35,000. In the spaces provided below, record the journal entry for the provision for uncollectible accounts under each of the following independent assumptions:

    a. The Allowance for Doubtful Accounts before adjustment has a credit balance of $500.

    b. The Allowance for Doubtful Accounts before adjustment has a debit balance of $250.

    c. Uncollectible accounts expense is estimated at 2% of sales.

68

WHAT-IF ANALYSIS

5. Erase the aging information for October and enter the following information for November 30, 2000:

Customer	Total	Not Yet Due	1–30 Days Past Due	31–60 Days Past Due	61–90 Days Past Due	Over 90 Days Past Due
A. J. Point	$ 2,850	$ 1,700	$ 800	$ 350		
C. Kyriakou	2,500	2,500				
ITT Tech	6,500	1,500	1,500	1,500	$1,000	$1,000
Silver Screen	400					400
Stock & Well	3,020	1,500		500	320	700
Tab-U-Late	8,900	8,900				
Totals	$24,170	$16,100	$ 2,300	$ 2,350	$1,320	$2,100

Save the results as AGING5. Print the worksheet. Has the estimated total uncollectible accounts increased or decreased in November? Explain.

GRAPHICAL ANALYSIS

6. a. With AGING5 still on the screen, click the Chart sheet tab. Describe what is being plotted out on this chart.

    b. Open the AGING3 file and click the Chart sheet tab. Compare the pattern of this chart to the one for AGING5. Note any trends below.

When the assignment is complete, close the files without saving them again.

TICKLERS (optional)

Worksheet. Suppose that there had been one additional customer with a balance due at November 30. This customer was Rob Lab and it owed $1,300, which was not yet due. Alter the AGING5 worksheet to allow entry of this information and modify any affected formulas. Use the Print Preview command (File menu) to make sure that the worksheet will print neatly on one page, then print the worksheet. Save the completed file as AGINGT.

Chart. Using the AGING3 file, develop a 3-D column chart to show the total estimated uncollectible amounts (in dollars) for each age category. No Chart Data Table is needed; use B23 to B27 as the X-axis (or make up your own labels) and then holding down the CTRL key, select F23 to F27 as the range of values to be plotted. Put your name somewhere on the chart. Save the file again as AGING3. Print the chart.

	A	B	C	D	E	F	G
2				AGING			
3				Aging Accounts Receivable			
4							
5					Date:	October 31, 2000	
6							
7				Analysis of Accounts Receivable by Age			
8			Not	1-30	31-60	61-90	Over 90
9			Yet	Days	Days	Days	Days
10	Customer	Total	Due	Past Due	Past Due	Past Due	Past Due
11	A. J. Point	$1,800	$1,300	$350			$150
12	G. Shrub	3,750	2,800	950			
13	ITT Tech	5,000	1,500	1,500	1,000	1,000	
14	Oxford Inc.	1,900	1,900				
15	Silver Screen	400					400
16	Stock & Well	1,750		500	320	700	230
17	Totals	$14,600	$7,500	$3,300	$1,320	$1,700	$780
18							
19					Estimate of Probable		
20					Uncollectible Accounts Expense		
21				Total	Percent	Total	
22				Amount	Uncoll.	Uncoll.	
23		Not yet due		FORMULA1	1%	FORMULA7	
24		1-30 days past due		FORMULA2	3%	FORMULA8	
25		31-60 days past due		FORMULA3	5%	FORMULA9	
26		61-90 days past due		FORMULA4	10%	FORMULA10	
27		Over 90 days past due		FORMULA5	25%	FORMULA11	
28		Totals		FORMULA6		FORMULA12	
29							

70

P8 ☼ INVENTORY COST FLOW ASSUMPTIONS (FIFOLIFO)

LEARNING OBJECTIVES

- Calculate the cost of goods sold and ending inventory using the specific identification, FIFO, LIFO, and weighted average methods.
- Contrast the effect of each on income determination, taxes, and cash flow during periods of inflation, deflation, and stable prices.
- Identify the source and effect of inventory ("fictitious") profits.
- Identify the effect of last minute purchases on income determination.

PROBLEM DATA

Del Rio began Rio Enterprises on January 1 with 200 units of inventory. During the year 500 additional units were purchased, 500 units were sold, and Del ended the year with 200 units. Del is very satisfied with his first year of business although the cost of replacing his inventory rose continually throughout the year. The 500 units sold for a total of $320,000 and the 500 units purchased to replace them cost $256,000, so his cash account has increased by $64,000. Del is concerned however because he has three obligations yet to meet: taxes, dividends, and his wife. Federal and state income taxes will take 40% of his income. His investors are to receive dividends equal to half of any income after taxes are paid. And finally, Del promised his wife a big trip to Hawaii if she let him quit his job as a professor and start his own business. He promised her he'd "make at least $50,000 after taxes. That will give us $25,000 after paying off the investors."

Del kept fairly good records during the year and knows the specific cost of each inventory unit sold. He has prepared the following table to summarize his purchases and sales.

Purchase Date	Unit Quantity	Unit Cost	Total Cost	Specific Units Sold	Cost of Units Sold
Beginning	200	$400	$ 80,000	200	$ 80,000
Mar. 7	100	$440	$ 44,000	50	22,000
May 13	50	480	24,000		
Aug. 28	200	520	104,000	200	104,000
Nov. 20	150	560	84,000	50	28,000
Total purchased	500		256,000		
Total available	700		$ 336,000		
Sales	500			500	$234,000
Ending balance	200				

A quick calculation shows that Rio's net income will be $51,600 using specific costs for the inventory sold. Sales minus cost of goods sold equals gross profit ($320,000 - $234,000 = $86,000). Taxes to be paid are 40% ($86,000 × .4 = $34,400). Subtract taxes from gross profit to get net income ($86,000 - $34,400 = $51,600).

Next, Del calculates his ending cash balance. He currently has $64,000 from his sales less his inventory replacement purchases ($320,000 - $256,000 = $64,000). He needs to pay taxes ($34,400) and dividends to his investors ($51,600 × .5 = $25,800). Subtracting $34,400 and $25,800 from $64,000 leaves him with only $3,800. Yikes!

Del is shocked by the computations. He cannot figure out how he will ever explain to his wife that he has net income in excess of $50,000 and yet after paying off the investors he will have only $3,800 to show for it! Del knows you are taking an accounting class and comes to you for help.

REQUIRED

1. Del has heard that the choice of an inventory cost flow assumption can have a significant effect on net income and taxes. He asks you to show him the differences between the specific identification method and the cost flow assumptions of FIFO, LIFO, and weighted average. Review the worksheet FIFOLIFO that follows these requirements. Note that all of the problem data have been entered in the Data Section of the worksheet.

2. Using a pencil, fill in columns F and G in the Data Section of the worksheet printout at the end of this problem.

3. Use the spaces provided below to write the formulas for each of the cells requested in the worksheet. Be careful to write formulas 1 through 8 broadly enough to include different sales quantities (e.g., suppose all inventory was sold, or no inventory was sold).

    FORMULA1_____   FORMULA8_____

    FORMULA2_____   FORMULA9_____

    FORMULA3_____   FORMULA10_____

    FORMULA4_____   FORMULA11_____

    FORMULA5_____   FORMULA12_____

    FORMULA6_____   FORMULA13_____

    FORMULA7_____   FORMULA14_____

4. Start the spreadsheet program and open the file FIFOLIFO from the Student Disk. Fill in columns F and G in the Data Section. Then enter all 14 formulas where indicated on the worksheet. Enter your name in cell A1. Save the results as FIFOLIF4. Print the worksheet when done. *Check figure: FIFO net income (cell E36), $56,400.*

5.   Examine your completed worksheet and answer the following questions:

   a.   Which inventory cost flow assumption produces the most net income?

   b.   Which inventory cost flow assumption produces the least net income?

   c.   What caused the difference between your answers to (a) and (b) above?

   d.   Which inventory cost flow assumption produces the highest ending cash balance?

   e.   Which inventory cost flow assumption produces the lowest ending cash balance?

   f.   Does the assumption that produces the highest net income also produce the highest cash balance? Explain.

   g.   As you recall, Del originally used the specific identification method in his initial calculations when he projected $51,600 net income. According to Del's reckoning, that should have left him cash of $25,800 (50% of $51,600) after paying his investors. Why would he only have $3,800 left? Explain.

   h.   Which inventory cost flow assumption would you suggest Del use? Explain.

WHAT-IF ANALYSIS

6.   What changes would have taken place if Del's purchase prices had fallen rather than risen? To find out, enter the following values in cells C11 through C14 respectively: $390, 380, 370, and 360. Print the results. Explain what the changes are and why they have taken place.

7. Suppose Del's purchase prices had remained constant. Enter $400 in cells C11 through C14. Explain what changes take place and why.

8. Reset the purchase prices to their original values (cells C11 through C14). Suppose Del had purchased 250 units on November 20 rather than 150. Enter 250 in cell C14 and alter column G in the Data Section. Explain what happens to net income under each inventory cost flow assumption and why. Also, what "management" implications might this have for Del?

9. Reset the November 20 purchase to 150 units including column G. To test your formulas, suppose that Del had sold 600 units rather than 500. Sales now total $384,000. The extra units sold come from the May 13 purchase (25 units) and the November 20 purchase (75 units). Change cell B17 to 600 and cells D32 through G32 to $384,000. Alter columns E, F, and G in the Data Section to reflect the change. Your formulas should automatically redo the Calculations and Answer Sections. Print the results again.

GRAPHICAL ANALYSIS

10. Close the file without saving and open it again (FIFOLIF4). Click the Chart sheet tab. On the screen is a column chart showing ending inventory costs. During a deflationary period, which bar (A, B, or C) represents FIFO costing, which represents LIFO costing, and which represents weighted average? Explain your reasoning.

When the assignment is complete, close the file without saving it again.

TICKLERS (optional)

Worksheet. On January 4 following year-end, Rio Enterprises received a shipment of 60 units of product costing $580 each. These units had been ordered by Del in December and had been shipped to him on December 27. They were shipped F.O.B. shipping point. Revise the FIFOLIF4 worksheet to include this shipment. Use the Print Preview command (File menu) to make sure that the worksheet will print neatly on one page, then print the worksheet. Save the completed file as FIFOLIFT.

Chart. Using the FIFOLIF4 file, prepare a 3-D bar (stacked) chart showing the cost of goods sold and ending inventory under each of the four inventory cost flow assumptions. No Chart Data table is needed. Use the values in the Calculations Section of the worksheet for your chart. Put your name somewhere on the chart. Save the file again as FIFOLIF4. Print the chart.

	A	B	C	D	E	F	G
2				FIFOLIFO			
3				Inventory Cost Flow Assumptions			
4							
5	Data Section						
6							
7					Specific	FIFO	LIFO
8	Purchase	Unit	Unit	Total	Units	Units	Units
9	Date	Quantity	Cost	Cost	Sold	Sold	Sold
10	Beginning Balance	200	$400	$80,000	200		
11	Mar 7	100	$440	$44,000	50		
12	May 13	50	480	24,000			
13	Aug 28	200	520	104,000	200		
14	Nov 20	150	560	84,000	50		
15	Total purchased	500		256,000			
16	Total available	700		$336,000			
17	Sales	500			500	0	0
18	Ending balance	200			these totals must agree		
19					with cell B17		
20							
21	Calculations						
22							
23					Specific	FIFO	LIFO	Average
24	Cost of goods sold				FORM1	FORM2	FORM3	FORM4
25	Ending inventory cost				FORM5	FORM6	FORM7	FORM8
26	Total goods available				$0	$0	$0	$0
27							
28	Answer Section						
29							
30					Income Statement		
31					Specific	FIFO	LIFO	Average
32	Sales				$320,000	$320,000	$320,000	$320,000
33	Cost of goods sold				FORM9	FORM10	0	0
34	Gross profit				FORM11	FORM12	$0	$0
35	Taxes (40%)				FORM13	FORM14	0	0
36	Net income				$0	$0	$0	$0
37							
38							
39					Cash Flow Analysis		
40					Specific	FIFO	LIFO	Average
41	Sales				$320,000	$320,000	$320,000	$320,000
42	Less inventory replacement				(256,000)	(256,000)	(256,000)	(256,000)
43					$64,000	$64,000	$64,000	$64,000
44	Less taxes				0	0	0	0
45	Less dividends				0	0	0	0
46	Change in cash account				$0	$0	$0	$0
47							

P9 ✡ GROSS PROFIT METHOD (GP)

LEARNING OBJECTIVES

- Use the gross profit method to estimate ending inventory.
- Identify reasons for differences between book and physical inventories.
- Interpret trends in the gross profit ratio.
- Alter the worksheet to include a new input category.
- Create a chart demonstrating the relationship between gross profit percentage and estimated ending inventory.

PROBLEM DATA

On September 30, 2000, the general ledger of Listo Inc., which uses the calendar year as its accounting period, showed the following year-to-date account balances:

Sales	$650,000
Sales returns and allowances	17,000
Purchases	600,000
Purchases returns and allowances	22,000

The merchandise inventory account had a $95,050 balance on January 1, 2000. The historical gross profit percentage is 30%.

REQUIRED

1. Listo Inc. prepares quarterly financial statements and takes physical inventory once a year—at the end of the accounting period. In order to prepare the financial statements for the third quarter, the store needs to have an estimate of ending inventory. You have been asked to use the gross profit method to estimate the ending inventory. Review the worksheet called GP. Study it carefully because it may have a solution format somewhat different from the one shown in your textbook.

2. Using the spaces provided below, write the formulas where requested in the worksheet.

    FORMULA1_____   FORMULA5_____

    FORMULA2_____   FORMULA6_____

    FORMULA3_____   FORMULA7_____

    FORMULA4_____

3. Start the spreadsheet program and open the file GP from the Student Disk. Enter all the formulas where indicated on the worksheet. Enter your name in cell A1. Save your completed worksheet as GP3. Print the worksheet. *Check figure: Estimated ending inventory (cell D22), $229,950.*

WHAT-IF ANALYSIS

4. On December 31, 2000, the year-to-date account balances of selected accounts were as follows:

Sales	$981,000
Sales returns and allowances	26,000
Purchases	900,000
Purchases returns and allowances	30,000

    Estimated ending merchandise inventory at December 31, 2000 is $_____.

5. A physical count of merchandise inventory on December 31, 2000 revealed inventory costing $287,000. In the space below, list at least two possible reasons for this balance to be different from the estimate in requirement 4.

GRAPHICAL ANALYSIS

6. Click the Chart sheet tab. The line chart that appears plots quarterly sales and gross profit for all four quarters. Examine the pattern of behavior for these two items and comment on any favorable or unfavorable trends noted. What is happening to the gross profit ratio?

    When the assignment is complete, close the file without saving it again.

TICKLERS (optional)

Worksheet. At the present time, Listo Inc. includes payments for freight costs in the purchases account. On the advice of an accountant, Listo Inc. will establish a separate account for freight-in charges (also called transportation-in) in 2001. Modify the GP3 worksheet to accept this additional item of input. Then estimate ending merchandise inventory at March 31, 2001 using the following data:

Sales	$300,000
Sales returns and allowances	7,500
Purchases	225,000
Purchases returns and allowances	9,500
Freight-in	2,200
Beginning inventory (12/31/X4)	287,000
Gross profit percent (historical)	29%

Use the Print Preview command (File menu) to make sure that the worksheet will print neatly on one page, then print the worksheet. Save the completed file as GPT.

Chart. Using the GP3 file, create an XY chart for the GP3 worksheet that demonstrates the relationship between gross profit percentage and estimated ending inventory. Complete the Chart Tickler Data Table and use it as a basis for preparing the chart. Put your name somewhere on the chart. Save the file again as GP3. Print the chart.

	A	B	C	D
2	GP			
3	Gross Profit			
4				
5	Data Section			
6				
7	Sales		$650,000	
8	Sales returns and allowances		17,000	
9	Purchases		600,000	
10	Purchases returns and allowances		22,000	
11	Beginning inventory		95,050	
12	Gross profit percent (historical)		30%	
13				
14	Answer Section			
15				
16	Beginning inventory			FORMULA1
17	Net purchases			FORMULA2
18	Cost of goods available for sale			FORMULA3
19	Net sales		FORMULA4	
20	Estimated gross profit (in dollars)		FORMULA5	
21	Estimated cost of goods sold			FORMULA6
22	Estimated ending inventory			FORMULA7
23				

P10 ✵ DEPRECIATION (DEPREC)

LEARNING OBJECTIVES

- Compute depreciation using the straight-line, sum-of-the-years-digits, and double-declining-balance methods using formulas or the Excel functions =SLN, =SYD, =DDB.
- Identify patterns of depreciation over an asset's life.
- Interpret patterns of accumulated depreciation over an asset's life.
- Alter the worksheet to allow for the computation of partial year depreciation.
- Create a chart plotting annual depreciation under all three depreciation methods.

PROBLEM DATA

Progressive Production Company recently acquired a new machine at a cost of $266,000. The machine has an estimated useful life of four years and no salvage value.

REQUIRED

1.   Progressive buys equipment frequently and wants to print a depreciation schedule for each asset's life. Review the worksheet called DEPREC that follows these requirements. Since some assets acquired are depreciated by straight-line, others by sum-of-the-years-digits, and others by double-declining-balance, DEPREC shows all three methods. You are to use this worksheet to prepare depreciation schedules for the new machine.

2.   Using the spaces provided below, write the formulas requested. Be sure to use cell references wherever possible in your formulas instead of numbers. You should find the year numbers in column B helpful for some formulas. Your instructor will tell you whether you are to (1) construct your own formulas or (2) use =SLN, =SYD, and =DDB. FORMULA1 has been written both ways for you as an example. If you are writing your own formulas, use the following expression to compute the sum-of-the-years-digits: N×(N+1)/2 where N equals the estimated life. Assume that all assets acquired will have at least a three-year life. Note that all cells on the worksheet containing zeros have been preprogrammed to perform depreciation calculations.

=(E7-E8)/E9 or	
FORMULA1____**=SLN(E7,E8,E9)**_____	FORMULA5_____
FORMULA2_____	FORMULA6_____
FORMULA3_____	FORMULA7_____
FORMULA4_____	FORMULA8_____

81

FORMULA9_____   FORMULA11_____

FORMULA10_____   FORMULA12_____

3. Start the spreadsheet program and open the file DEPREC from the Student Disk. Enter the formulas in the appropriate cells. Does your depreciation total $266,000 under all three methods? If not, correct your error. *Hint:* If your double-declining-balance method is off, check cell E20 where FORMULA12 is located. It should include an =IF statement that will enter a modified calculation of depreciation if Year 4 is the last year of the asset's expected life. Enter your name in cell A1. Save the completed file as DEPREC3. Print the worksheet. *Check figure: DDB depreciation for Year 3 (cell E19), $33,250.*

4. In the space below, prepare the journal entry to record the depreciation taken in Year 3 under the sum-of-the-years-digits method.

WHAT-IF ANALYSIS

5. To test your formulas, assume the machine purchased above had an estimated useful life of three years. Enter the new information in the Data Section of the worksheet. Does your depreciation total $266,000 under all three methods?

    There are four common errors made by students completing this worksheet. Let's clear up three of them. One, an asset that has a three-year life should have no depreciation claimed in Year 4. This can be corrected using an =IF statement in Year 4. See Appendix A of *Excel Quick* for a discussion of this function. For example, the correct formula in cell C20 is =IF(B20>E9,0,(E7-E8)/E9) or =IF(B20>E9,0,SLN(E7,E8,E9)). Use this example to correct all the other formulas for Year 4. You may wish to edit what you have already entered rather than retype them.

    Two, the sum-of-the-years-digits calculation is dependent on the life of the asset and on which year it is. In formulas 4–8, the values 4, 3, 2, and 1 work when the asset has a four-year life, but not when it has a three-year life. If you used these values in your original formulas, change them to the more general form of E9, (E9-1), (E9-2), and so forth.

    Three, as mentioned in requirement 3, the double-declining-balance calculation needs to be modified in the last year of the asset's life. Assuming you have already modified the formula for Year 4 (per instructions in requirement 3), alter the formula for Year 3 also.

    If you corrected any formulas, test their correctness by trying different estimated useful lives (between 3 and 10) in cell E9. Then reset the Data Section to the original values, save the revised file as DEPREC3, and reprint the worksheet to show the correct formulas.

The fourth common error doesn't need to be corrected in this problem. The general form of the double-declining-balance formula needs to be modified to check the net book value of the asset each year to make sure it does not go below salvage value. =DDB does this automatically, but if you are writing your own formulas, this gets very complicated and is beyond the scope of the problem.

6. As another test of your formulas, enter a salvage value of $20,000 in cell E8. Test your model with both the three-year and four-year estimated useful lives. Does your depreciation total $246,000 under all three methods? Print the worksheet. If necessary, correct any errors in your formulas and redo DEPREC3 again. *Check figure: Using a four-year life and $20,000 salvage value, DDB depreciation in Year 3 (cell E19) is $33,250.*

7. A machine was recently bought for $335,000 with a salvage value of $30,000 and estimated useful life of ten years. Enter the new information in the Data Section of the worksheet. Again make sure the totals for all three methods are in agreement. Print the worksheet. Save this new data as DEPREC7.

GRAPHICAL ANALYSIS

8. The double-declining-balance method is often claimed to be the method providing the highest initial depreciation expense. This is generally true for the first few years of an asset's life, but what if a company wants to use a method that will maximize depreciation charges over an extended period of time? Is double-declining-balance still best?

Open the DEPREC7 file. Click the Chart sheet tab. This chart shows accumulated depreciation under all three depreciation methods over the ten-year life of the machine purchased in requirement 7. Approximately how long does the double-declining-balance method provide the highest accumulated write-offs?

Now let's change the scenario slightly. What happens if you change estimated salvage value from $30,000 to zero? To find out, press any key and then enter 0 in cell E8. Click the Chart tab again. Approximately how long does double-declining-balance provide the highest accumulated write-offs in this case?

Is double-declining-balance always the best method to maximize depreciation charges? Explain.

When the assignment is complete, close the file without saving it again.

TICKLERS (optional)

Worksheet. The problem thus far has assumed that assets are depreciated a full year in the year acquired. Normally, depreciation begins in the month acquired. For example, an asset acquired at the beginning of April is depreciated for only nine months in the year of acquisition. Modify the DEPREC3 worksheet to include the month of acquisition as an additional item of input. To demonstrate proper handling of this factor on the depreciation schedule, modify the formulas for the first two years. Be careful because some of the formulas for the second year may not actually need to be revised to provide the correct second-year depreciation. Do not modify the formulas for Years 3 through 10 and ignore the numbers shown in those years. They will be incorrect as will be the totals. Use the Print Preview command (File menu) to make sure that the worksheet will print neatly on one page, then print the worksheet. Save the completed file as DEPRECT.

Hint: Insert the month in row 10 of the Data Section specifying the month by a number (e.g., April is the fourth month of the year). Redo the formulas in rows 17 and 18.

Chart. Using the DEPREC7 file, prepare a line chart or XY chart that plots annual depreciation expense under all three depreciation methods. No Chart Data Table is needed; use the range B17 to E26 on the Worksheet as a basis for preparing the chart if you prepare an XY chart. Use C17 to E26 if you prepare a line chart. Put your name somewhere on the chart. Save the file again as DEPREC7. Print the chart.

	A	B	C	D	E
2			*DEPREC*		
3			*Depreciation*		
4					
5	Data Section				
6					
7			Cost of asset		$266,000
8			Estimated salvage value		$0
9			Estimated useful life in years		4
10					
11	Answer Section				
12					
13			Depreciation Expense		
14				Sum of	Double
15			Straight	Years	Declining
16		Year	Line	Digits	Balance
17		1	FORMULA1	FORMULA5	FORMULA9
18		2	FORMULA2	FORMULA6	FORMULA10
19		3	FORMULA3	FORMULA7	FORMULA11
20		4	FORMULA4	FORMULA8	FORMULA12
21		5	0	0	0
22		6	0	0	0
23		7	0	0	0
24		8	0	0	0
25		9	0	0	0
26		10	0	0	0
27		Total	$0	$0	$0
28					

P11 ☼ PAYROLL REGISTER (PR)

LEARNING OBJECTIVES

- Prepare and use a payroll register including social security and medicare withholdings.
- Use =IF and =ROUND to design the social security tax and union dues formulas.
- Record journal entries for payroll, employer's tax liability, and payment of payroll taxes.
- Identify behavior patterns among payroll taxes over time.
- Alter the worksheet to include an additional employee.
- Create a chart showing the percentage of an employee's gross pay that is withheld for taxes, etc., and how much is left over as net pay.

PROBLEM DATA

Design World has five employees, and they are paid at the end of each month. Payroll data for November are as follows:

Employee	Gross Pay for November	Federal Income Tax Withheld	Cumulative Gross Pay to October 31
Anders	$9,000	$2,500	$?
Brayer	1,530	302	15,570
Jacobs	1,210	266	6,550
Malone	8,837	2,385	88,370
Wilson	4,200	1,355	55,000

Other information (using 1999 rates) is as follows:

a. Social security taxes are 6.2% on monthly gross pay up to a cumulative total pay of $72,600 for each employee per year.
b. Medicare taxes are 1.45% on monthly gross pay with no upper limit.
c. A $25 monthly deduction is made for union dues for all union members.
d. Unemployment taxes are paid on monthly gross pay up to the first $7,000 earned by each employee each year. State and federal rates are 2.7% and 0.8%, respectively.

REQUIRED

1. Based on the 1999 tax rates provided above, use a calculator to compute how much would be withheld from Anders' November paycheck in the following three cases (round to the nearest penny):

Cumulative Gross Pay to October 31	Social Security	Medicare	Insurance
$50,000	_____	_____	_____
$70,000	_____	_____	_____
$90,000	_____	_____	_____

2.   You have been asked to record the November payroll information using a payroll register and a general journal. Review the printout of the worksheet PR, a computerized payroll register, that follows these requirements. The columns will automatically retotal as new entries are made. Entries in column B indicate whether or not employees are union members. Assume Anders' cumulative gross pay to October 31 could be $50,000, $70,000, or $90,000.

3.   To make the worksheet reusable each month, the social security tax formulas should be designed to automatically compute whether (1) full tax is due, (2) no tax is due (e.g., cumulative gross pay is over the ceiling), or (3) some tax is due. =IF statements will be required. Also, the =ROUND function should be used for formulas 1 through 3 to eliminate rounding errors. FORMULA2 has been provided for you below. Review Appendix A of *Excel Quick* and explain the meaning of each part of the formula.

|—(a)—|——(b)——|—————————(c)——————————|—(d)—|(e)|

FORMULA2:   =ROUND(IF(I14>G25,0,IF((I14+C14)>G25,(G25-I14)*G23,C14*G23)),2)

a.

b.

c.

d.

e.

4.   In the spaces provided below, write the other formulas requested. FORMULA4 should also use the =IF function.

FORMULA1_____

FORMULA3_____

FORMULA4_____

FORMULA5_____

5.   Start the spreadsheet program and open the file PR from the Student Disk. Enter the month in cell E7. Enter the gross pay and federal income tax withheld for each employee and enter

$50,000 for Anders' cumulative gross pay (cell I13). Then, enter the formulas where indicated on the worksheet. As the formulas are entered, the cells that contain zeros will automatically be filled. Enter your name in cell A1. Save the completed file as PR5. Print the worksheet when done. *Check figure: Total net pay (cell H18), $16,571.44.*

WHAT-IF ANALYSIS

6.   Verify that your formulas for Anders' work by entering $70,000 and $90,000 for cumulative gross pay in cell I13. Compare your withholding amounts to your answers in requirement 1. Correct your formulas if necessary and save the file as PR5 again.

7.   In the space provided below, prepare the journal entry to record the November payroll for *all* employees assuming that the payroll is paid on November 30 and that Anders' cumulative gross pay (cell I13) is $70,000.

8.   In the space provided below, prepare the journal entry as of November 30 to record the employer's payroll tax accrual for November. Also prepare the journal entries to record the payment of all payroll taxes and union dues, assuming that they are all due on December 15.

9.   **Optional:** Revise the data in rows 22–25 using updated tax information for your current year. This will be provided by your instructor. Save the revised file as PR9. Print the worksheet when done.

GRAPHICAL ANALYSIS

10. Click the Chart sheet tab. On the screen is a chart of the four payroll taxes that Design World incurs during each year. By the behaviors shown on the chart, identify below which of the four expenses each represents.

A _____

B _____

C _____

D _____

When the assignment is complete, close the file without saving it again.

TICKLERS (optional)

Worksheet. A new employee was hired during November and was mistakenly omitted from the payroll register. The employee's last name is Yeoman, and his gross pay for November is $1,300. Add the new employee to the PR5 worksheet and include all standard withholding rates in computing net pay. Federal income tax withheld is $175. He is a union member. Use the Print Preview command (File menu) to make sure that the worksheet will print neatly on one page, then print the worksheet. Save the completed file as PRT.

Chart. Using the PR5 file, prepare a 3-D pie chart to show the percentage of an employee's gross pay that is withheld for taxes, social security, etc., and how much is left over as net pay. Use Jacobs as your example. Complete the Chart Tickler Data Table and use it as a basis for preparing the chart. Put your name somewhere on the chart. Save the file again as PR5. Print the chart.

	A	B	C	D	E	F	G	H	I
2					*PR*				
3					*Payroll Register*				
4									
5					Design World				
6					Payroll Register				
7					November				
8									
9					Deductions				
10				Federal	Social				Cum.
11			Gross	Income	Seucrity	Medicare	Union		Gross Pay
12	Employee	U	Pay	Tax	Tax	Tax	Dues	Net Pay	to Oct 31
13	Anders	Y			FORM1	FORM3	FORM4	FORM5	?
14	Brayer	N			FORM2	0.00	0.00	0.00	15,570
15	Jacobs	Y			0.00	0.00	0.00	0.00	6,550
16	Malone	N			0.00	0.00	0.00	0.00	88,370
17	Wilson	N			0.00	0.00	0.00	0.00	55,000
18			0.00	0.00	0.00	0.00	0.00	0.00	
19									
20									
21					Tax Information				
22					Current Year		1999		
23					FICA tax rate		6.20%		
24					Medicare tax rate		1.45%		
25					FICA tax maximum income		$72,600		
26									

91

P12 ☆ PARTNERSHIP (PARTNER)

LEARNING OBJECTIVES

- Compute the partner's share of profit or loss based on salary allowances, interest allowances, and stated ratios.
- Evaluate the partnership profit-sharing ratios.
- Alter the worksheet to include different residual profit-sharing ratios.
- Create a chart showing the relationship between net income amounts and profit sharing by the partners.

PROBLEM DATA

Anthony Richards and Sonia Singh recently formed a partnership. Richards, who quit his old job in order to form the partnership, invested $41,000 cash, which was most of his life's savings. Singh invested $35,000 of assets and $24,000 cash. She will work part-time for the business. The partners are trying to find an equitable way of dividing net income to take into account that Singh invested more capital, but Richards will spend twice as much time as Singh in running the business. The only agreement the partners have made is to divide equally any excess or deficit that is present after allowances for salary and interest. They expect net income in the first year to be $75,000, although it could range anywhere from $50,000 to $100,000. Richards has suggested the following method of dividing net income:

Interest on original investments at 10%

Salary allowances: Richards $40,000
                 Singh   20,000

REQUIRED

1. The partners would like you to experiment with different methods of dividing income to determine the effect of various interest rates, various salary allowances, and various levels of partnership income. The worksheet PARTNER has been provided to assist you in performing this analysis.

2. Using the spaces provided below, write the formulas where requested in the worksheet.

FORMULA1_____   FORMULA4_____

FORMULA2_____   FORMULA5_____

FORMULA3_____   FORMULA6_____

3.	Start the spreadsheet program and open the file PARTNER from the Student Disk. Enter all formulas where indicated on the worksheet. Cells that contain zeros on the worksheet have been preprogrammed. As formulas are entered, these zeros will be replaced by values. When you are finished, make sure that total net income (cell D21) is equal to the actual net income (cell B12). Enter your name in cell A1. Save the file as PARTNER3. Print the worksheet. *Check figure: Richards' share of net income (cell B25), $46,600.*

WHAT-IF ANALYSIS

4.	In the table below, record Richards' and Singh's shares if net income is $75,000. Then use your model to calculate each partner's share if the net income of the partnership is $50,000 and if it is $100,000. Write the answers in the table below.

Richards' Plan

Net income	$50,000	$75,000	$100,000
Richards' share	$_____	$_____	$_____
Singh's share	$_____	$_____	$_____

5.	Singh does not like Richards' proposed method for dividing net income, so she has suggested that net income be divided in the following manner:

Interest on original investments at 20%
Salary allowances:	Richards	$30,000
			Singh		15,000

Calculate each partner's share under Singh's plan for $50,000, $75,000, and $100,000 of partnership net income. Write the results in the table below.

Singh's Plan

Net income	$50,000	$75,000	$100,000
Richards' share	$_____	$_____	$_____
Singh's share	$_____	$_____	$_____

6.	What factors should Richards and Singh consider to help them reach an agreement?

GRAPHICAL ANALYSIS

7.   Reset the Data Section to its initial values. Click the Chart sheet tab. This chart is based on the problem data. Answer the following questions about the chart:

   a.   What is the title for the X-axis?

   b.   What does the A data range represent?

   c.   What does the B data range represent?

   d.   What is a good title for this chart?

   When the assignment is complete, close the file without saving it again.

TICKLERS (optional)

Worksheet. Assume that the partners want to consider different profit-sharing arrangements for the excess other than a 50–50 split. Modify the Data Section and the Answer Section of PARTNER3 so that the effect of different sharing arrangements (e.g., 60%–40%, 90%–10%) can be examined. Note that this change will not in any way affect the formulas for the salary or interest allowances. When you are done, set the Data Section for a 60–40 split in favor of Richards and save the completed file as PARTNERT. Write your revised FORMULA5 and FORMULA6 below. Use the Print Preview command (File menu) to make sure that the worksheet will print neatly on one page, then print the worksheet.

   FORMULA5_____

   FORMULA6_____

Chart. Fix up the chart in the PARTNER3 file by adding the appropriate titles, legends, and formats. Put your name somewhere on the chart. Save the file again as PARTNER3. Print the chart.

	A	B	C	D
2	PARTNER			
3	Partnership			
4				
5	Data Section			
6				
7	Interest on original investment	10%		
8	Original investment - Richards	$41,000		
9	Original investment - Singh	59,000		
10	Salary allowance - Richards	40,000		
11	Salary allowance - Singh	20,000		
12	Net income	75,000		
13				
14	Answer Section			
15				
16	Division of net income	Richards	Singh	Total
17	Salary allowance	FORMULA1	FORMULA2	$0
18	Interest allowance	FORMULA3	FORMULA4	0
19	Total	$0	$0	$0
20	Excess of income over allowances	FORMULA5	FORMULA6	0
21	Net income allocation	$0	$0	$0
22				

P13 ☼ BOND PRICING AND AMORTIZATION (BONDS)

LEARNING OBJECTIVES

- Calculate bond issuance prices (with detailed assistance) and develop amortization schedules. Record entries for bond issuance and interest expense using both the straight-line and effective interest method of amortization.
- Calculate bond prices after issuance.
- Interpret the relationship between bond prices and years to maturity.
- Alter the worksheet to accommodate bonds with up to twenty years maturity.
- Create a chart plotting the annual interest expense under both the straight-line and effective interest methods.

PROBLEM DATA

Universal Enterprises recently issued $1,000,000 of 10-year, 8% bonds at an effective interest rate of 9%. Bond interest is payable annually.

REQUIRED

1. You have been asked to calculate the issuance price of the bonds and prepare amortization schedules for any discount or premium. The worksheet BONDS has been provided to assist you. Note that the worksheet contains a scratch pad at the bottom which has been preprogrammed to automatically compute and display the relevant cash flows needed for bond pricing.

2. The bond pricing formula utilizes the Net Present Value function on your spreadsheet program. The formula is broken into two parts as identified by the letters in parentheses above the formula. See Appendix A in *Excel Quick* for a discussion on the NPV function, and then explain the meaning of each part of the formula.

|————(a)————|————(b)————|

FORMULA1:   =NPV(E10,C60:C71)+NPV(E10,D60:D71)

a.

b.

3. Using the spaces provided, write the formulas required to complete the worksheet. Assume all bonds have at least a two-year maturity. Year 0 is the date of issuance. Bond discount (column E) should be a negative number, and bond premium should be a positive number. The amortization of bond discount (column C in the straight-line table and column D in the effective interest table) should be a positive number, and the amortization of bond premium should be a negative number.

FORMULA2_____   FORMULA14_____

FORMULA3_____   FORMULA15_____

FORMULA4_____   FORMULA16_____

FORMULA5_____   FORMULA17_____

FORMULA6_____   FORMULA18_____

FORMULA7_____   FORMULA19_____

FORMULA8_____   FORMULA20_____

FORMULA9_____   FORMULA21_____

FORMULA10_____   FORMULA22_____

FORMULA11_____   FORMULA23_____

FORMULA12_____   FORMULA24_____

FORMULA13_____   FORMULA25_____

4. Start the spreadsheet program and open the file BONDS from the Student Disk. Enter the formulas in the appropriate cells. Enter your name in cell A1. Save the file as BONDS4. Print the worksheet when done. *Check figures: Bond issue price (cell F17), $935,823; Bond carrying value for Year 10 (cells F32 and F49), $1,000,000.*

5. Prepare journal entries in the space provided below to record (a) the issuance of the bond, (b) the interest payment and required amortization for Year 1 using the straight-line method of amortization, and (c) the interest payment and required amortization for Year 1 using the effective interest method of amortization.

WHAT-IF ANALYSIS

6. Use the worksheet to compute the bond issue price and amortization schedules if the effective interest rate is 7%. Save the file as BONDS6. Print the worksheet when done. Also, repeat requirement 5 in the space provided below for this bond.

7. Use the worksheet to compute the bond issue price if the effective interest rate is 8%.

   Bond issue price $_____

8. Find the effective interest rate for $5,000,000 of 6-year, 8% bonds (interest payable annually), which were issued for $5,189,490. To do this, enter the known information in the Data Section and experiment with different effective interest rates until you get a bond price of exactly $5,189,490. (You may have to use an effective interest rate with decimals.) Print the worksheet when done.

GRAPHICAL ANALYSIS

9. a. Reset the Data Section to its initial values. The price of this bond is $935,823. What would it be if there were only 9 or 8 years to maturity? Use the worksheet to compute the bond issue prices and enter them below.

   Bond issue price (9 years to maturity) $_____
   Bond issue price (8 years to maturity) $_____

   b. Compare these prices to the bond-carrying values found in the effective interest amortization schedule you originally printed out in requirement 4. Explain the similarity.

   c. Click the Chart sheet tab. The chart presented shows the price behavior of this bond based on years to maturity. Explain what effect years to maturity has on bond prices. Check your explanation by trying 7% as the effective rate (cell E10) and clicking the Chart sheet tab again. Also, try 8%.

   When the assignment is complete, close the file without saving it again.

TICKLERS (optional)

Worksheet. Modify the BONDS4 worksheet to accommodate bonds with up to twenty-year maturities. Use your new model to determine the issue price and amortization schedules of a $2,000,000, 18-year, 9% bond issued to yield 10%. Use the Print Preview command (File menu) to make sure that the worksheet will print neatly, then print the worksheet. Save the completed file as BONDST.

Hint: Expand both amortization schedules to twenty years. Expand the scratch pad to twenty years. Modify FORMULA1 in cell F17 to include the new ranges.

Chart. Using the BONDS4 file, prepare a line chart that plots annual interest expense over the ten-year life of this bond under both the straight-line and effective interest methods. No Chart Data Table is needed. Put A23 to A32 in the Label format and then select A23 to A32, D23 to D32, and B40 to B49 as a collection. Enter all appropriate titles, legends, formats, and so forth. Put your name somewhere on the chart. Save the file again as BONDS4. Print the chart.

	A	B	C	D	E	F
2			BONDS			
3			Bond Pricing and Amortization			
4						
5		Data Section				
6						
7		Face value of bond			$1,000,000	
8		Years to maturity *			10	
9		Stated interest rate			8.0%	
10		Effective interest rate			9.0%	
11						
12		* Worksheet is designed for use with bonds having a maturity of				
13		12 years or less and paying interest annually.				
14						
15		Answer Section				
16						
17		Bond issue price				FORMULA1
18						
19			Amortization Schedule - Straight Line Method			
20		Cash		Interest	(Disc.)	Bond
21	Year	Paid	Amortization	Expense	Premium	Carrying Value
22	0				FORMULA2	FORMULA3
23	1	FORMULA4	FORMULA5	FORMULA6	FORMULA7	FORMULA8
24	2	FORMULA9	FORMULA10	FORMULA11	FORMULA12	FORMULA13
25	3	0	0	0	0	0
26	4	0	0	0	0	0
27	5	0	0	0	0	0
28	6	0	0	0	0	0
29	7	0	0	0	0	0
30	8	0	0	0	0	0
31	9	0	0	0	0	0
32	10	0	0	0	0	0
33	11	0	0	0	0	0
34	12	0	0	0	0	0
35						
36			Amortization Schedule - Effective Interest Method			
37		Interest	Cash		(Disc.)	Bond
38	Year	Expense	Paid	Amortization	Premium	Carrying Value
39	0				FORMULA14	FORMULA15
40	1	FORMULA16	FORMULA17	FORMULA18	FORMULA19	FORMULA20
41	2	FORMULA21	FORMULA22	FORMULA23	FORMULA24	FORMULA25
42	3	0	0	0	0	0
43	4	0	0	0	0	0
44	5	0	0	0	0	0
45	6	0	0	0	0	0
46	7	0	0	0	0	0
47	8	0	0	0	0	0
48	9	0	0	0	0	0
49	10	0	0	0	0	0
50	11	0	0	0	0	0
51	12	0	0	0	0	0
52						

	B	C	D
56	Scratch Pad		
57	Display of relevant cash flows		
58		Annual	Bond
59	Year	Interest	Maturity
60	1	80000	0
61	2	80000	0
62	3	80000	0
63	4	80000	0
64	5	80000	0
65	6	80000	0
66	7	80000	0
67	8	80000	0
68	9	80000	0
69	10	80000	1000000
70	11	0	0
71	12	0	0

P14 ☆ CONSOLIDATIONS (CONS)

LEARNING OBJECTIVES

- Prepare a worksheet for a consolidated balance sheet at acquisition date.
- Prepare elimination entries for consolidation.
- Contrast the effects of purchase and pooling-of-interests accounting.
- Interpret the effect of consolidation on various accounts.
- Alter the worksheet to include minority interest.
- Create a chart contrasting the asset composition of the parent and subsidiary companies.

PROBLEM DATA

On July 31, 2000, B Corporation issued 10,000 shares of its own $5 par common stock for all of D Incorporated's outstanding shares of common stock. The fair market value of the B Corporation stock is $28 per share. The balance sheets of the two companies on July 31, immediately after the acquisition, are as follows:

	B Corp.	D Inc.
Assets		
Cash	$ 54,600	$ 19,550
Notes receivable	55,000	3,000
Accounts receivable	74,000	37,300
Interest receivable	3,000	0
Inventories	121,300	30,450
Prepaid expenses	11,500	8,400
Investment in D Inc.	280,000	0
Land	62,000	28,000
Buildings and equipment (net)	210,000	130,000
	$871,400	$256,700
Liabilities & Stockholders' Equity		
Notes payable	$ 5,000	$ 40,000
Accounts payable	96,400	44,700
Dividends payable	25,000	0
Interest payable on notes	0	2,000
Common stock, $5 par	325,000	0
Common stock, $8 par	0	96,000
Paid in capital in excess of par	250,000	0
Retained earnings	170,000	74,000
	$871,400	$256,700

All of D Incorporated's notes payable are owed to B Corporation.

REQUIRED

1.   You have been asked to prepare a worksheet for a consolidated balance sheet as of July 31. Review the worksheet called CONS that has been provided to assist you. The column totals will change as eliminations are made. The zeros in the consolidated balance sheet column have been preprogrammed, and as formulas are entered on the worksheet these zeros will be replaced by values. Note that there is a row for entering Goodwill on the worksheet. Some textbooks suggest using goodwill, others don't. Use the method shown in your textbook.

2.   In the space provided below, write the elimination entries required to prepare the consolidated balance sheet. Identify each elimination entry by a separate letter (e.g., journal entry a, journal entry b, etc.). Assume that the business combination has been recorded as a purchase. The fair value of D Incorporated's assets correspond to the book carrying amounts except for land, which is valued at $100,000 for consolidation purposes.

3.   Using the spaces provided below, write the formulas requested in the worksheet. Note that the elimination amounts are to be entered in columns E and G of the worksheet. FORMULA1 has been provided for you as an example.

FORMULA1___=B13+C13+E13-G13___   FORMULA4_____

FORMULA2_____   FORMULA5_____

FORMULA3_____   FORMULA6_____

4.   Start the spreadsheet program and open the file CONS from the Student Disk. Complete the worksheet by entering the formulas and proper eliminations. Also in columns D and F, enter the letter corresponding to each journal entry you used in requirement 2. Enter your name in cell A1. Save the completed file as CONS4. Print the worksheet when done. *Check figure: Total consolidated assets (cell H23), $916,100.*

WHAT-IF ANALYSIS

5.   Assume that the company wished to treat the consolidation as a pooling of interest. How would such treatment have affected B Corporation's balance sheet on July 31? D Incorporated's balance sheet? The consolidated balance sheet?

Redo the B Corporation balance sheet assuming that the consolidation had qualified as a pooling of interest. Also, redo the eliminating entries on the worksheet to reflect pooling of interest. Save your answer as CONS5. Print the worksheet when done.

GRAPHICAL ANALYSIS

6.   Close the CONS5 file and open CONS4. Click the Chart sheet tab. This is a graphical representation of some of the accounts of B Corporation and D Incorporated before and after consolidation. Identify in the spaces provided below the accounts represented by the letters on the X-axis.

A

B

C

D

E

F

When the assignment is complete, close the file without saving it again.

TICKLERS (optional)

Worksheet. Assume that when B Corporation issued its 10,000 shares, it only bought 80% of D Incorporated. Modify the CONS4 worksheet to include minority interest and redo the elimination entries on the worksheet to reflect this new scenario. Use the Print Preview command (File menu) to make sure that the worksheet will print neatly on one page, then print the worksheet. Save the completed file as CONST.

Chart. Using the CONS4 file, prepare a 3-D stacked column chart comparing the total cash, notes receivable, and accounts receivable balances of B Corporation with those of D Incorporated. No Chart Data Table is needed; use the range A13 to C15 as a basis for preparing the chart. Enter all appropriate titles, legends, and formatting on the chart. Put your name somewhere on the chart. Save the file again as CONS4. Print the chart.

	A	B	C	D	E	F	G	H
2			CONS					
3			Consolidations					
4								
5			B Corp. & D Inc.					
6			Work Sheet for Consolidated Balance Sheet					
7			July 31, 2000					
8								
9								
10								Consolidated
11					Eliminations			Balance
12		B Corp.	D Inc.		Debit		Credit	Sheet
13	Cash	$54,600	$19,550					FORMULA1
14	Notes receivable	55,000	3,000					FORMULA2
15	Accounts rec.	74,000	37,300					FORMULA3
16	Interest rec.	3,000	0					0
17	Inventories	121,300	30,450					0
18	Prepaid expenses	11,500	8,400					0
19	Investment in D	280,000	0					0
20	Land	62,000	28,000					0
21	Net build & equip.	210,000	130,000					0
22	Goodwill							0
23	Totals	$871,400	$256,700					$0
24								
25	Notes payable	$5,000	$40,000					FORMULA4
26	Accounts payable	96,400	44,700					FORMULA5
27	Dividends payable	25,000	0					FORMULA6
28	Interest pay/notes	0	2,000					0
29	Common stock, $5	325,000						0
30	Common stock, $8		96,000					0
31	Paid in capital	250,000	0					0
32	Retained earnings	170,000	74,000					0
33	Totals	$871,400	$256,700		$0		$0	$0
34								

P15 ✧ STATEMENT OF CASH FLOWS (CASHFLOW)

LEARNING OBJECTIVES

- Prepare a worksheet for the statement of cash flows.
- Prepare a statement of cash flows.
- Interpret cash flow trends from operating, investing, and financing activities.
- Alter the worksheet to include a statement of cash flows.
- Create a chart illustrating the historical relationship between operating cash flows and net income.

PROBLEM DATA

The comparative balance sheet of Creative Concepts Corporation at June 30, the end of the fiscal year, is as follows:

Creative Concepts Corporation
Comparative Balance Sheet
June 30, 2001 and 2000

Assets	2001	2000
Cash	$ 57,210	$ 39,600
Accounts receivable	131,250	112,215
Merchandise inventory	200,100	210,930
Prepaid expenses	10,350	10,875
Plant assets	460,500	315,000
Accumulated depreciation—plant assets	(128,550)	(90,000)
Total assets	$730,860	$598,620
Liabilities & Stockholders' Equity		
Accounts payable	$ 61,110	$ 59,220
Dividends payable	54,000	30,000
Bonds payable	120,000	105,000
Common stock, $20 par	240,000	210,000
Premium on common stock	33,000	22,500
Retained earnings	222,750	171,900
Total liabilities & stockholders' equity	$730,860	$598,620

Additional data obtained from the records of Creative Concepts Corporation are as follows:

a.   Net income for fiscal 2001 was $104,850.
b.   Depreciation reported on income statement for fiscal 2001 was $46,500.

107

c.   Purchased $165,000 of new equipment, putting $90,000 cash down and issuing $75,000 of bonds for the balance.

d.   Old equipment originally costing $19,500, with accumulated depreciation of $7,950, was sold for $13,500.

e.   Retired $60,000 of bonds.

f.   Declared cash dividends of $54,000.

g.   Issued 1,500 shares of common stock at $27 cash.

REQUIRED

1.   You have been asked to prepare a statement of cash flows for Creative Concepts Corporation. Review the worksheet called CASHFLOW that has been provided to assist you in preparing the statement. The worksheet has been designed so that as you make entries in columns D and F, column G will be automatically updated. Columns C and E are to be used to enter letter references for each of the debit and credit entries on the worksheet.

2.   Using the spaces provided below, write the formulas requested in the worksheet. FORMULA1 has been provided for you as an example.

FORMULA1____=B17+D17-F17____   FORMULA4_____

FORMULA2_____   FORMULA5_____

FORMULA3_____   FORMULA6_____

3.   Start the spreadsheet program and open the file CASHFLOW from the Student Disk. First, enter the formulas. Then, complete the worksheet in the manner described below.

According to the problem, cash increased from $39,600 to $57,210 during the year. This is a $17,610 increase. To record this increase on the worksheet, move to row 17. Since this is the first account you are analyzing, enter the letter **a** in column C. Then enter **17610** in column D (a debit since cash increased). This brings the year-end balance (column G) to $57,210, its proper balance.

Now move to the bottom part of the statement where you see the categories Operating Activities, Investing Activities, etc. The credit side of the entry has to be entered here.

The proper space for this cash entry is on row 58. Enter the letter **a** in cell E58 and **17610** in cell F58. Notice the totals at the bottom of the page (row 59) now agree.

The next account balance that changed is accounts receivable. It increased by $19,035. To enter this change on the worksheet, enter the letter **b** in cell C18 and **19035** in cell D18 (again a debit since accounts receivable increased). This brings the year-end balance in column G to $131,250, its proper balance. The change in accounts receivable balance is an operating activity adjustment (as explained in your textbook). Enter the credit side of this entry in cells E34 and F34, and enter the explanation **Increase in accounts receivable** in cell A34. *Note:* Your textbook probably shows "Net income" as the first item under Operating Activities. We will get to that later. The sequence in which you enter items on this worksheet is not important.

All other balance sheet accounts must be analyzed in the same manner, placing appropriate debit or credit entries in the top part of the worksheet to obtain the proper balances in column G, and then entering the second side of the entry in the appropriate row on the bottom part of the worksheet. You should use letter references to identify all entries. Also, you must enter a description of the entry in column A under the appropriate activity category. Although a sequence of analyzing the balance sheet from top to bottom is suggested here, this order is not necessary. As mentioned above, your textbook may specify a different sequence. Also, note that some accounts may have both debit and credit adjustments to them.

The worksheet is not a substitute for a statement of cash flows, but it does provide you with all the numbers you need to properly prepare one.

You will be done with your analysis when:

a.   The individual account balances at June 30, 2001, as shown on the worksheet (column G) equal those shown in the problem data above.

b.   The transaction column totals are equal (cells D59 and F59).

When you are finished, enter your name in cell A1. Save your completed file as CASHFLO3. Print the worksheet when done. *Check figure: Total credits at 6/30/2001 (cell G31) $859,410.*

4.   In the space provided on the next page, prepare a statement of cash flows in good form using the indirect method. Use the format shown in your textbook.

WHAT-IF ANALYSIS

5.   Suppose that an audit of Creative Concepts Corporation encountered the following two errors:

a.   An accounts receivable totaling $4,500 should have been written off as a bad debt at the end of the year. Year-end accounts receivable should be only $126,750.

b.   The $54,000 dividend declared at year-end had in fact been paid. Thus, both the cash account and the dividends payable account are overstated at year-end.

Correct both errors on the worksheet. Save your completed file as CASHFLO5. Print the worksheet when done.

Creative Concepts Corporation
Statement of Cash Flows
For the Year Ended June 30, 2001

GRAPHICAL ANALYSIS

6.   Click the Chart sheet tab. On the chart, the components of cash flow for Creative Concepts Corporation over the last five years are plotted. Comment below on the behavior of each component. Do you see favorable trends? Unfavorable ones?

         When the assignment is complete, close the file without saving it again.

TICKLERS (optional)

Worksheet. Place a formal statement of cash flows (see requirement 4) on the CASHFLO3 worksheet. Use columns I through O for your statement. Put your name at the top. Print your work (select and print just the statement of cash flow cells). Use the Print Preview command (File menu) to make sure that the statement (not the worksheet) will print neatly on one page, then print it out. Save the completed file as CASHFLOT.

Chart. Using the CASHFLO3 file, prepare a 2-D line chart which illustrates the relationship between operating cash flows and net income over the last five years. Use the appropriate columns on the Chart Data Table as a basis for preparing the chart. Use all appropriate titles, legends, formatting, etc. Put your name somewhere on the chart. Save the file again as CASHFLO3. Print the chart.

	A	B	C	D	E	F	G
1							
2		**CASHFLOW**					
3		*Statement of Cash Flow*					
4							
5		Creative Concepts Corporation					
6		Work Sheet for Statement of Cash Flows					
7		For Year Ended June 30, 2001					
8							
9							
10				Analysis of			
11				Transactions for			
12				Year Ended 6/30/01			
13			Account				Account
14			Balance				Balance
15			6/30/00		Debit	Credit	6/30/01
16	Debits						
17	Cash		39,600				**FORMULA1**
18	Accounts receivable		112,215				**FORMULA2**
19	Merchandise inventory		210,930				**FORMULA3**
20	Prepaid expenses		10,875				0
21	Plant assets		315,000				0
22	Total		688,620				0
23	Credits						
24	Accumulated depreciation		90,000				**FORMULA4**
25	Accounts payable		59,220				**FORMULA5**
26	Dividends payable		30,000				**FORMULA6**
27	Bonds payable		105,000				0
28	Common stock, $20 par		210,000				0
29	Premium on common stock		22,500				0
30	Retained earnings		171,900				0
31	Total		688,620				0
32							

	A	B	C	D	E	F	G
33	Operating Activities						
34							
35							
36							
37							
38							
39							
40							
41							
42							
43	Investing Activities						
44							
45							
46							
47							
48	Financing Activities						
49							
50							
51							
52							
53							
54	Noncash Investing & Financing						
55							
56							
57					0		0	
58	Change in cash						
59					0		0	
60							

P16 ✿ RATIO ANALYSIS (RATIOA)

LEARNING OBJECTIVES

- Using ten key ratios, perform standard analysis on a company over a three-year period.
- Interpret the results and compare them to industry norms.
- Contrast rate of return on assets with rate of return on equity.
- Alter the worksheet to include two additional ratios.
- Create a chart contrasting the quick (acid test) and current ratios.

PROBLEM DATA

The comparative financial statements of New World Technology are as follows:

New World Technology
Comparative Income Statement
For Years Ended December 31, 2000 and 1999

	2000	1999
Net sales	$ 3,516,075	$ 3,300,330
Cost of merchandise sold	2,820,000	2,550,000
Gross profit	$ 696,075	$ 750,330
Selling expenses	$ 123,000	$ 127,500
General expenses	81,660	88,500
Total operating expenses	$ 204,660	$ 216,000
Operating income	$ 491,415	$ 534,330
Other expense (interest)	36,000	19,500
Income before income tax	$ 455,415	$ 514,830
Income tax	164,400	220,905
Net income	$ 291,015	$ 293,925

New World Technology
Comparative Retained Earnings Statement
For Years Ended December 31, 2000 and 1999

	2000	1999
Retained earnings, January 1	$ 1,420,095	$1,186,170
Net income for year	291,015	293,925
Total	$ 1,711,110	$ 1,480,095
Common stock dividends	82,500	60,000
Retained earnings, December 31	$ 1,628,610	$ 1,420,095

New World Technology
Comparative Balance Sheet
December 31, 2000 and 1999

Assets		2000		1999
Cash	$	34,830	$	63,000
Accounts receivable		232,500		298,575
Merchandise inventory		825,480		637,500
Prepaid expenses		22,500		25,500
Plant assets (net)		1,800,000		1,530,000
Total assets		$2,915,310		$2,554,575
Liabilities & Stockholders' Equity				
Accounts payable	$	326,400	$	39,180
Bonds payable, 10% due 2010		360,000		195,000
Total liabilities	$	686,400	$	534,180
Common stock	$	600,300	$	600,300
Retained earnings		1,628,610		1,420,095
Total stockholders' equity		$2,228,910		$2,020,395
Total liabilities & stockholders' equity		$2,915,310		$2,554,575

REQUIRED

1. Review the worksheet RATIOA that follows these requirements. You have been asked to perform a ratio analysis of this company for 2000.

2. In the spaces provided below, write the formulas requested.

FORMULA1_____   FORMULA6_____

FORMULA2_____   FORMULA7_____

FORMULA3_____   FORMULA8_____

FORMULA4_____   FORMULA9_____

FORMULA5_____   FORMULA10_____

3. Start the spreadsheet program and open the file RATIOA from the Student Disk. Enter the formulas in the appropriate cells. Enter your name in cell A1. Save the completed model as RATIOA3. Print the worksheet when done. *Check figure: Acid test (quick) ratio (cell C58), .82.*

116

4.   a.   What information does a comparison of the current ratio and acid test ratio provide?

     b.   Is the company using leverage to its advantage? Explain.

     c.   What other observations can be made comparing New World Technology's ratios to the following industry norms:

Acid test ratio	1.0
Current ratio	2.0
Accounts receivable turnover	12.0
Inventory turnover	4.0
Gross profit ratio	40%
Net income to sales	7%
Rate earned on total assets	12%
Rate earned on common stock equity	20%
Debt to total assets	.35
Times interest earned	8

WHAT-IF ANALYSIS

5.   Prepare a ratio analysis for New World Technology for 2001. The following information is available for 2001:

Accounts payable	$ 342,240	Income tax	$ 135,300
Accounts receivable	206,400	Merchandise inventory	814,500
Bonds payable	360,000	Net sales	3,753,000
Cash	?	Other expenses (interest)	36,000
Common stock	600,300	Plant assets	2,025,000
Common stock dividends	102,000	Prepaid expenses	4,500
Cost of goods sold	3,102,000	Selling expenses	132,000
General expenses	84,750		

The 2001 information should be entered in column B of the RATIOA3 worksheet. The 2000 information should be entered in column C. Save the revised file as RATIOA5. Print the worksheet when done.

117

6.   Compare your printout from requirement 3 with your printout from requirement 5. From these two sets of ratios, what conclusions can be drawn concerning changes from 2000 and 2001?

GRAPHICAL ANALYSIS

7.   With the 2001 data still on the screen, click the Chart sheet tab. The chart presented shows the rates of return for New World Technology for the last five years. Answer the following questions:

a.   In 1997, the rate of return on assets exceeded the rate of return on common stockholders' equity. Why might this have occurred? Be as specific as possible.

b.   Is the company better off in 2001 than it was in 1997? Why or why not?

When the assignment is complete, close the file without saving it again.

TICKLERS (optional)

Worksheet. Modify the RATIOA5 worksheet to have it compute two additional activity ratios: number of days' sales in receivables and number of days' sales in merchandise inventory. Use the 2000 and 2001 data and assume a 365-day year. Write out the formulas for your ratios below.

Days' sales in receivables_____
Days' sales in inventory_____

Use the Print Preview command (File menu) to make sure that the worksheet will print neatly, then print the worksheet. Save the completed file as RATIOAT.

Chart. Using the RATIOA5 file, prepare a 3-D column chart that compares the acid test and current ratios for New World Technology for 2000 and 2001. Complete the Chart Tickler Data Table and use it as a basis for preparing the chart. Enter all appropriate titles, legends, and formats. Put your name somewhere on the chart. Save the file again as RATIOA5. Print the chart.

	A	B	C
2	**RATIOA**		
3	*Ratio Analysis*		
4			
5	Data Section		
6			
7	New World Technology		
8	Comparative Income Statement		
9	For Years Ended December 31, 2000 and 1999		
10		2000	1999
11	Net sales	$3,516,075	$3,300,330
12	Cost of merchandise sold	2,820,000	2,550,000
13	Gross profit	$696,075	$750,330
14	Selling expenses	$123,000	$127,500
15	General expenses	81,660	88,500
16	Total operating expenses	$204,660	$216,000
17	Operating income	$491,415	$534,330
18	Other expenses (interest)	36,000	19,500
19	Income before income tax	$455,415	$514,830
20	Income tax	164,400	220,905
21	Net income	$291,015	$293,925
22			
23			
24	New World Technology		
25	Comparative Retained Earnings Statement		
26	For Years Ended December 31, 2000 and 1999		
27		2000	1999
28	Retained earnings, January 1	$1,420,095	$1,186,170
29	Net income for year	291,015	293,925
30	Total	$1,711,110	$1,480,095
31	Common stock dividends	82,500	60,000
32	Retained earnings, December 31	$1,628,610	$1,420,095
33			
34			
35	New World Technology		
36	Comparative Balance Sheet		
37	As of December 31, 2000 and 1999		
38	Assets	2000	1999
39	Cash	$34,830	$63,000
40	Accounts receivable	232,500	298,575
41	Merchandise inventory	825,480	637,500
42	Prepaid expenses	22,500	25,500
43	Plant assets (net)	1,800,000	1,530,000
44	Total assets	$2,915,310	$2,554,575
45			
46	Liabilities & Stockholders' Equity		
47	Accounts payable	$326,400	$339,180
48	Bonds payable, 10% due 2010	360,000	195,000
49	Total liabilities	$686,400	$534,180
50	Common stock	$600,300	$600,300
51	Retained earnings	1,628,610	1,420,095
52	Total stockholders' equity	$2,228,910	$2,020,395
53	Total liabilities & stockholders' equity	$2,915,310	$2,554,575
54			

	A	B	C
55	Answer Section		
56			
57	Liquidity ratios:		
58	Acid-test (quick) ratio		FORMULA1
59	Current ratio		FORMULA2
60	Activity ratios:		
61	Accounts receivable turnover		FORMULA3
62	Inventory turnover		FORMULA4
63	Profitability ratios:		
64	Gross profit ratio		FORMULA5
65	Net income to sales		FORMULA6
66	Rate earned on total assets		FORMULA7
67	Rate earned on common stock equity		FORMULA8
68	Coverage ratios:		
69	Debt to total assets		FORMULA9
70	Times interest earned		FORMULA10
71			
72			

P17 ☼ MANUFACTURING ACCOUNTING (MFG)

LEARNING OBJECTIVES

- Prepare a schedule of cost of goods manufactured and sold.
- Calculate changes in labor cost needed to achieve production goals.
- Alter the worksheet to include an income statement for a manufacturing firm.
- Create a chart showing the dollar amount of materials, labor, and overhead.

PROBLEM DATA

The following information is for Jackson Manufacturing for the year ended December 31, 2000:

Depreciation—equipment	$ 45,000
Direct labor	642,000
Direct materials inventory, 1/1/00	91,500
Direct materials inventory, 12/31/00	93,000
Factory rent	76,410
Finished goods, 1/1/00	132,000
Finished goods, 12/31/00	172,500
Indirect labor	37,500
Indirect materials	26,250
Purchases of direct materials	645,180
Work in process, 1/1/00	30,300
Work in process, 12/31/00	28,665

REQUIRED

1. You have been asked to prepare a schedule of cost of goods manufactured and sold for the year just ended. Review the worksheet MFG that follows these requirements.

2. Using the spaces provided, write the formulas and titles where requested.

FORMULA1_____   FORMULA5_____

FORMULA2_____   FORMULA6_____

FORMULA3_____   FORMULA7_____

FORMULA4_____   FORMULA8_____

FORMULA9_____ FORMULA11_____

FORMULA10_____ FORMULA12_____

TITLE A_____ TITLE E_____

TITLE B_____ TITLE F_____

TITLE C_____ TITLE G_____

TITLE D_____ TITLE H_____

3. Start the spreadsheet program and open the file MFG from the Student Disk. Enter the formulas and titles where requested on the worksheet. The cells that contain zeros now will change to non-zero values as formulas are entered. Enter your name in cell A1. Save the file as MFG3. Print the worksheet when done. *Check figure: Cost of goods sold (cell D46), $1,431,975.*

WHAT-IF ANALYSIS

4. The following data pertains to 2001 activities of Jackson Manufacturing:

Depreciation—equipment	$ 46,500
Direct labor	664,500
Direct materials inventory, 12/31/01	85,050
Factory rent	81,000
Finished goods, 12/31/01	181,500
Indirect labor	42,000
Indirect materials	30,000
Purchases of direct materials	603,300
Work in process, 12/31/01	27,225

Use your completed worksheet to determine the firm's cost of goods sold for 2001. Remember to change the year in row 24. Save the 2001 file as MFG4. Print the worksheet when done.

If sales and other expenses were identical in 2000 and 2001, during which year did Jackson earn more income? Why?

GRAPHICAL ANALYSIS

5. Open MFG3 and click the Chart sheet tab. The management of Jackson is convinced that the quality of their products is highly dependent on their relative labor costs. Experience has shown that direct labor should account for at least 45% of the total product cost. From the pie chart that appears on the screen, Jackson did not achieve this goal in 2000. How much should Jackson have spent on direct labor to reach its 45% goal?

To find out, try different values for direct labor (cell C8), clicking the Chart sheet tab after each attempt. When you find a direct labor level that increases the direct labor percentage to 45%, enter the answer below:

In 2000, direct labor needed to be $_____.

Open MFG4 and click the Chart sheet tab. Did Jackson achieve its 45% goal in 2001? If not, answer the following:

In 2001, direct labor needed to be $_____.

When the assignment is complete, close the files without saving them again.

TICKLERS (optional)

Worksheet. The MFG3 worksheet presents the company's manufacturing activities for 2000. The company also had the following selling and general activities in 2000: sales of $3,375,750, selling expenses of $600,000, and general expenses of $300,000. Modify the worksheet to include this information in the Data Section and change the Answer Section so that it is in the form of an income statement. Use the Print Preview command (File menu) to make sure that the worksheet will print neatly on one page, then print the worksheet. Save the completed file as MFGT.

Hint: Expand the Data Section to include these additional input items alphabetically. Insert a row for sales under the heading in the Answer Section. Add the rest of the income statement information to the bottom of the schedule. You will need to enter formulas for gross profit, all the expenses, and net income. You will also need to change the statement name.

Chart. Using the MFG3 file, prepare a 3-D bar chart to show the dollar amount of materials, labor, and overhead incurred by Jackson in 2000 and 2001. Complete the Chart Data Table and use it as a basis for preparing the chart. Enter all appropriate titles, legends, and formats. Put your name somewhere on the chart. Save the file again as MFG3. Print the chart.

	A	B	C	D
2		*MFG*		
3		*Manufacturing Accounting*		
4				
5		Data Section		
6				
7	Depreciation--equipment		$45,000	
8	Direct labor		642,000	
9	Direct materials inventory, 1/1		91,500	
10	Direct materials inventory, 12/31		93,000	
11	Factory rent		76,410	
12	Finished goods, 1/1		132,000	
13	Finished goods, 12/31		172,500	
14	Indirect labor		37,500	
15	Indirect materials		26,250	
16	Purchases of direct materials		645,180	
17	Work in process, 1/1		30,300	
18	Work in process, 12/31		28,665	
19				
20		Answer Section		
21				
22		Jackson Manufacturing		
23		Schedule of Cost of Goods Manufactured and Sold		
24		For the Year Ended December 31, 2000		
25				
26	Direct materials			
27	Direct materials inventory, 1/1			$91,500
28	Add: TITLE A			FORMULA1
29	Cost of direct materials available			$0
30	Less: TITLE B			FORMULA2
31	Cost of direct materials used			FORMULA3
32	Direct labor			642,000
33	Manufacturing overhead:			
34	Factory rent		$76,410	
35	TITLE C		FORMULA4	
36	TITLE D		FORMULA5	
37	TITLE E		FORMULA6	0
38	Total manufacturing costs			FORMULA7
39	Work in process, 1/1			30,300
40	Total work in process available			$0
41	Less: TITLE F			FORMULA8
42	Cost of goods manufactured			FORMULA9
43	TITLE G			FORMULA10
44	Cost of goods available for sale			FORMULA11
45	Less: Finished goods, 12/31			172,500
46	TITLE H			FORMULA12
47				

124

P18 ☼ PROCESS COSTING (PPRCSS)

LEARNING OBJECTIVES

- Compute equivalent units of production and unit costs using FIFO.
- Prepare two cost of production reports and make comparisons.
- Use the results of unit cost computations in tracing the flow of costs through the accounts.
- Alter the worksheet by rearranging the Data and Answer Sections.
- Create a chart showing the relative proportion of materials and conversion costs per equivalent unit.

PROBLEM DATA

The following information is provided for Porter Enterprises for the month of June. All materials are added to production at the beginning of the manufacturing process, and conversion costs are incurred uniformly throughout manufacturing. Porter uses the FIFO inventory method.

	Units	Cost
Work in process, 6/1/00 (40% completed)	60,000	$ 94,800
Materials added during June		150,000
Conversion costs incurred during June		600,000
Units completed during June	210,000	
Work in process, 6/30/00 (70% completed)	30,000	

REQUIRED

1. You have been asked to prepare a cost of production report for the month of June. The worksheet PPRCSS contains all of the problem data in the Data Section and a partially completed cost of production report in the Answer Section. Study the Answer Section carefully to make sure that you understand the five-step format used by Porter for its cost of production report. (Production cost report formats vary a great deal from company to company.)

2. Using the spaces provided below, write the 16 formulas requested. FORMULA3 has been done for you as an example.

FORMULA1_____   FORMULA4_____

FORMULA2_____   FORMULA5_____

FORMULA3_____ =D9*(1-C9) _____   FORMULA6_____

FORMULA7_____   FORMULA12_____

FORMULA8_____   FORMULA13_____

FORMULA9_____   FORMULA14_____

FORMULA10_____   FORMULA15_____

FORMULA11_____   FORMULA16_____

3. Start the spreadsheet program and open the file PPRCSS from the Student Disk. Enter the formulas where indicated on the worksheet. Enter your name in cell A1. Save your completed model as PPRCSS3. Print the worksheet when done. *Check figure: Materials cost per equivalent unit (cell E50), $.83.*

WHAT-IF ANALYSIS

4. Test your worksheet with the following data for the month of July. Save your results as PPRCSS4. Use the print macro to print the results.

	Units	Cost
Work in process, 7/1/00 (70% completed)	30,000	$ 85,870
Materials added during July		162,000
Conversion costs incurred during July		432,000
Units completed during July	172,500	
Work in process, 7/31/00 (30% completed)	37,500	

5. In the space provided below, record the journal entry to transfer the completed goods from work in process to finished goods for the month of July.

GRAPHICAL ANALYSIS

6. The owners of Porter Enterprises keep very close tabs on their manufacturing costs. Assuming the quality of the product is unchanged from June to July, in which month is cost efficiency the best? To find out, open the PPRCSS3 file and click the Chart sheet tab. Review the chart and write your conclusions below. Verify your observations by reviewing the printouts of PPRCSS3 and PPRCSS4.

When the assignment is complete, close the file without saving it again.

TICKLERS (optional)

Worksheet. Revise the PPRCSS3 worksheet to put the Answer Section on top and the Data Section on the bottom. Use the Print Preview command (File menu) to make sure that the worksheet will print neatly on two pages, then print the worksheet. Save the completed file as PPRCSST.

Chart. Using the PPRCSS3 file, prepare a 3-D pie chart that discloses the relative proportion of materials and conversion costs per equivalent unit in June. No Chart Data Table is needed; use E49 to F50 as a basis for preparing your chart. Enter all appropriate titles, legends, and formats. Put your name somewhere on the chart. Save the file again as PPRCSS3. Print the chart.

	A	B	C	D	E	F
2			**PPRCSS**			
3			*Process Costing*			
4						
5	Data Section					
6						
7			Percent			
8			Completed	Units	Cost	
9	Work in process, beginning		40%	60,000	$94,800	
10	Materials added				150,000	
11	Conversion costs incurred				600,000	
12	Units completed during month			210,000		
13	Work in process, ending		70%	30,000		
14						
15	Answer Section					
16						
17			Porter Enterprises			
18			Cost of Production Report			
19			For Month of June 2000			
20						
21			Step 1: Units to Account For			
22						
23	Beginning work in process	60,000		Units completed		210,000
24	Units started	FORMULA1		Ending work in process		30,000
25	Total units to be accounted for	0		Total units accounted for		240,000
26						
27						
28			Step 2: Costs to Account For			
29						
30	Beginning work in process			$94,800		
31	Materials added			150,000		
32	Conversion costs incurred			600,000		
33	Total costs			$844,800		
34						

	A	B	C	D	E	F
35						
36			Step 3: Equivalent Unit Computations			
37						
38				Total	Equivalent units	
39				Units	Materials	Conversion
40	Beginning work in process			60,000	FORMULA2	FORMULA3
41	Units started and completed			FORMULA4	FORMULA5	FORMULA6
42	Ending work in process			30,000	FORMULA7	FORMULA8
43	Total units (must agree with step 1)			0		
44	Total equivalent units				0	0
45						
46						
47			Step 4: Costs Per Equivalent Unit			
48						
49					Materials	Conversion
50	Cost per equivalent unit (rounded to nearest cent)				FORMULA9	FORMULA10
51						
52	Total unit cost (materials + conversion)					FORMULA11
53						
54						
55			Step 5: Production Cost Allocation			
56						
57	Beginning work in process:					
58	Prior period cost				FORMULA12	
59	Conversion of beginning work in process				FORMULA13	$0
60	Units started and completed					FORMULA14
61	Ending work in process:					
62	Materials				FORMULA15	
63	Conversion				FORMULA16	
64	Total ending work in process					0
65	Total costs accounted for (must agree with step 2)					$0
66						

P19 ✿ COST-VOLUME-PROFIT ANALYSIS (CVP)

LEARNING OBJECTIVES

- Develop a cost-volume-profit analysis model.
- Calculate contribution margin, contribution margin ratio, break-even point, and projected income.
- Determine the effect of changes in price, variable costs, and fixed costs.
- Interpret the information provided by cost-volume-profit charts.
- Alter the worksheet to include an income statement in contribution margin format.
- Create a profit/volume chart.

PROBLEM DATA

Condor Manufacturing, which maintains the same level of inventory at the end of each year, provided the following information about expenses anticipated for 2001:

	Fixed Expenses	Variable Expenses (per unit sold)
Production costs:		
Direct materials		$ 4.30
Direct labor		4.70
Factory overhead	$225,000	3.00
Selling expenses:		
Sales salaries and commissions	97,000	.75
Advertising	47,500	
Miscellaneous selling expense	16,200	
General expenses:		
Office salaries	87,000	
Supplies	12,300	1.25
Miscellaneous general expense	15,000	
	$500,000	$14.00

The selling price of Condor's single product is $20. In recent years, profits have fallen and Condor's management is now considering a number of alternatives. For 2001, Condor wants to have a net income of $200,000, but expects to sell only 90,000 units unless some changes are made.

REQUIRED

1. The president of Condor has asked you to calculate the company's projected net income (assuming 90,000 units are sold) and the sales needed to achieve the company's net income objective for 2001. Also, compute Condor's contribution margin per unit, contribution margin ratio, and break-even point for 2001. The worksheet CVP has been provided to assist you. Note that the data from the problem have already been entered into the Data Section of the worksheet.

2. In the spaces provided below, write the seven formulas requested in the worksheet.

    FORMULA1_____   FORMULA5_____

    FORMULA2_____   FORMULA6_____

    FORMULA3_____   FORMULA7_____

    FORMULA4_____

3. Start the spreadsheet program and open the file CVP from the Student Disk. Enter the formulas where indicated on the worksheet. Enter your name in cell A1. Save the solution as CVP3 and print the worksheet. *Check figure: Break-even point in sales dollars (cell C34), $1,666,667.*

4. Based on Condor's current situation, will it earn its target net income? If not, how many units need to be sold to achieve the target? Explain.

WHAT-IF ANALYSIS

5. The president of Condor would like to know the effect that each of the following suggestions for improving performance would have on contribution margin per unit, sales needed to break even, and projected net income for 2001. Each change should be considered independently. Reset the Data Section to its original values after each suggestion is analyzed. Fill in the table following the suggestions with the results of your analysis.

    a. The president suggests cutting the product's price. Since the market is relatively sensitive to price, ". . . a 10% cut in price ought to generate a 30% increase in sales. How can you lose?"

    b. The sales manager feels that putting all sales personnel on straight commission would help. This would eliminate $77,000 in fixed sales salaries expense; variable sales commissions would increase to $2.00 per unit. This move would also increase sales volume by 30%.

132

c.   Condor's head of product engineering wants to redesign the package for the product. This will cut $1.00 per unit from direct materials and $0.50 per unit from direct labor, but will increase fixed factory overhead by $10,000 for additional depreciation on the new packaging machine. The package redesign would not affect sales volume.

d.   The firm's consumer marketing manager suggests undertaking a new advertising campaign on cable TV. This would cost $30,000 more than is currently planned for advertising but would be expected to increase sales volume by 30%.

e.   The production superintendent suggests raising quality and raising price. This will increase direct materials by $1.00 per unit, direct labor by $0.50 per unit, and fixed factory overhead by $40,000. With improved quality, ". . . raise the price to $22 and advertise the heck out of it. If you double your current planned advertising, I'll bet you can increase your sales volume by 30%."

	Contribution Margin per Unit	Break-even Point (units)	Projected Net Income
original data	_____	_____	_____
a.	_____	_____	_____
b.	_____	_____	_____
c.	_____	_____	_____
d.	_____	_____	_____
e.	_____	_____	_____

6.   From the analysis above, should Condor use any of the suggestions?

7.   The president of Condor can't figure out where his math went wrong. Explain it to him. Also compute how many units would have to be sold at $18 in order for the firm to achieve its target net income of $200,000.

GRAPHICAL ANALYSIS

8.   Reset the Data Section to its initial values and click the Chart sheet tab. On the screen you will see a cost-volume-profit chart (also commonly called a break-even chart). In the space provided below, identify the names of the data ranges.

Data range A _____

Data range B _____

Data range C _____

Use the chart to answer the following questions:

a.   What is the approximate break-even point in units?

b.   What is the approximate profit or loss if Condor sells 40,000 units?

c.   What dollar amount of fixed factory overhead would push the break-even point to 100,000 units? (*Hint:* enter different amounts in cell B11 and click the Chart sheet tab until the desired result is achieved.)

d.   What selling price would push the break-even point to 100,000 units?

When the assignment is complete, close the file without saving it again.

TICKLERS (optional)

Worksheet. Condor's controller would like to have the worksheet display an income statement in a contribution margin format (Sales – variable costs = contribution margin – fixed costs = net income). Using the CVP3 file, begin the statement in column E. Use the Print Preview command (File menu) to make sure that the statement will print neatly on one page, then print the statement. Save the completed file as CVPT.

Chart. Using the CVP3 file, create a line chart in which profit or loss is plotted on the Y-axis and sales volume is plotted on the X-axis. This is commonly called a profit/volume chart. Although sales volume can be expressed in either units or dollars, use units for your chart. Revise the Chart Data Table to include a column for profits. Use this table as a basis for preparing the chart. Put your name somewhere on the chart. Save the file again as CVP3. Print the chart.

	A	B	C
2	CVP		
3	Cost-Volume-Profit Analysis		
4			
5	Data Section		
6			
7		Fixed	Variable
8	Production costs		
9	Direct materials		$4.30
10	Direct labor		4.70
11	Factory overhead	$225,000	3.00
12	Selling expenses		
13	Sales salaries & commissions	97,000	0.75
14	Advertising	47,500	
15	Miscellaneous selling expense	16,200	
16	General expenses		
17	Office salaries	87,000	
18	Supplies	12,300	1.25
19	Miscellaneous general expense	15,000	
20		$500,000	$14.00
21			
22	Projected unit sales		90,000
23	Selling price per unit		$20.00
24	Target net income		$200,000
25			
26	Answer Section		
27			
28	Contribution margin per unit		FORMULA1
29	Contribution margin ratio		FORMULA2
30			
31	Break-even point (units)		FORMULA3
32	Target net income (units needed to achieve)		FORMULA4
33			
34	Break-even point (sales dollars)		FORMULA5
35	Target net income (sales dollars needed to achieve)		FORMULA6
36			
37	Projected net income		FORMULA7
38			

P20 ☼ VARIABLE COSTING (VARCOST)

LEARNING OBJECTIVES

- Prepare variable costing and absorption costing income statements.
- Reconcile the differences between absorption and variable costing net income.
- Contrast the effects of production levels on absorption and variable costing net income.
- Alter the worksheet to allow it to handle sales in excess of production.
- Create a chart plotting absorption costing income and variable costing income.

PROBLEM DATA

The records of Modern Industrial contain the following information for the month of August:

Actual production in units	100,000
Sales in units	80,000
Sales price per unit	$30
Variable manufacturing cost per unit	14
Variable selling expense per unit	2
Fixed manufacturing cost	630,000
Fixed selling expenses	100,000

The company has no beginning inventory.

REQUIRED

1. You have been asked to prepare a variable costing (direct costing) income statement and an absorption costing income statement for the month of August. Review the worksheet VARCOST that follows these requirements.

2. Using the spaces provided below, write the 10 formulas requested. FORMULA1 has been written for you as an example.

FORMULA1_____**=B8*B9**_____   FORMULA6_____

FORMULA2_____   FORMULA7_____

FORMULA3_____   FORMULA8_____

FORMULA4_____   FORMULA9_____

FORMULA5_____   FORMULA10_____

3. Start the spreadsheet program and open the file VARCOST from the Student Disk. Enter the formulas where indicated on the worksheet. Enter your name in cell A1. Save the completed file as VARCOST3. Print the worksheet when done. *Check figure: Absorption income (cell C31), $516,000.*

4. In the space below, explain why the operating income calculated by the absorption method is not the same as that calculated by the variable cost method.

WHAT-IF ANALYSIS

5. To determine the effect of different levels of production on the company's income, move to cell B7 (Actual Production). Change the number in B7 to the different production levels given in the table below. The first level, 100,000, is the current level. What happens to operating income on both statements as production levels change? Enter the operating incomes in the table below.

August Operating Income	Production Level 100,000	Production Level 90,000	Production Level 80,000
Absorption	$_____	$_____	$_____
Variable	$_____	$_____	$_____

Does the level of production affect income under either costing method? Explain your findings.

GRAPHICAL ANALYSIS

6. Click the Chart sheet tab. This chart is based on the problem data and the two income statements. Answer the following questions about the chart:

   a. What is the title for the X-axis?

   b. What is the title for the Y-axis?

   c. What does data range A represent?

d.   What does data range B represent?

e.   Why do the two data ranges cross?

f.   What would be a good title for this chart?

When the assignment is complete, close the file without saving it again.

TICKLERS (optional)

Worksheet. The VARCOST3 worksheet is capable of calculating variable and absorption income when unit sales are equal to or less than production. An equally common situation (that this worksheet cannot handle) is when beginning inventory is present and sales volume exceeds production volume. Revise the worksheet Data Section to include:

Beginning inventory in units	15,000
Beginning inventory cost (absorption)	$304,500
Beginning inventory cost (variable)	$210,000

Also, change actual production to 70,000.

Revise the Answer Section to accommodate this new data. Assume that Modern Industrial uses the weighted average costing method for inventory. Use the Print Preview command (File menu) to make sure that the worksheet will print neatly on one page, then print the worksheet. Save the completed file as VARCOSTT. *Check figure: Absorption income, $338,118.*

Chart. Using the VARCOST3 file, fix up the chart used in requirement 6 by adding appropriate titles and legends and formatting the X- and Y-axes. Put your name somewhere on the chart. Save the file again as VARCOST3. Print the chart.

	A	B	C
2	**VARCOST**		
3	*Variable Costing*		
4			
5	Data Section		
6			
7	Actual production in units	100,000	
8	Sales in units	80,000	
9	Sales price per unit	$30	
10	Variable manufacturing costs per unit	$14	
11	Variable selling costs per unit	$2	
12	Fixed manufacturing costs	$630,000	
13	Fixed selling expenses	$100,000	
14			
15	Answer Section		
16			
17	Income statement: Absorption costing		
18			
19	Sales		FORMULA1
20	Cost of goods sold:		
21	Variable manufacturing costs	FORMULA2	
22	Fixed manufacturing costs	FORMULA3	
23	Total goods available for sale	$0	
24	Less ending inventory	FORMULA4	
25	Cost of goods sold		0
26	Gross profit		$0
27	Selling expenses:		
28	Fixed selling expenses	FORMULA5	
29	Variable selling expenses	FORMULA6	
30	Total selling expenses		0
31	Operating income		$0
32			
33			
34	Income statement: Variable costing		
35			
36	Sales		$0
37	Cost of goods sold:		
38	Variable manufacturing costs	FORMULA7	
39	Less ending inventory	FORMULA8	
40	Variable cost of goods sold		0
41	Manufacturing margin		$0
42	Variable selling expenses		FORMULA9
43	Contribution margin		$0
44	Fixed costs:		
45	Fixed manufacturing costs	FORMULA10	
46	Fixed selling expenses	0	
47	Total fixed costs		0
48	Operating income		$0
49			

P21 ☆ MASTER BUDGET (MASTER)

LEARNING OBJECTIVES

- Develop a master budget including a balance sheet, income statement, and cash budget.
- Interpret the budgets and the differences between profit and cash flow.
- Contrast the effects of changes in projected sales on the budgets.
- Alter the worksheet by adding a column to show quarterly totals.
- Create a chart showing projected sales.

PROBLEM DATA

Quest Industries has provided the following information at May 31, 2001:

Unit Sales, 2001

April	1,500	actual
May	1,000	actual
June	1,600	budgeted
July	1,400	budgeted
August	1,500	budgeted
September	1,200	budgeted

Balance Sheet, May 31, 2001

Cash	$ 8,000
Accounts receivable	107,800
Merchandise inventory	52,800
Fixed assets (net)	130,000
Total assets	$298,600
Accounts payable (merchandise)	$ 74,800
Owner's equity	223,800
Total liabilities and equity	$298,600

Other information:

Average selling price, $98
Average purchase price per unit, $55
Desired ending inventory, 60% of next month's unit sales
Collections from customers:

In month of sale	20%
In month after sale	60%
Two months after sale	20%

Projected cash payments:
        Inventory purchases are paid for in month following acquisition.
        Variable cash expenses, other than inventory, are equal to 30% of each month's
        sales and are paid in month of sale.
        Fixed cash expenses are $10,000 per month and are paid in month incurred.
Depreciation on equipment is $1,000 per month.

REQUIRED

1.   You have been asked to prepare a master budget for the upcoming quarter (June, July, and
        August). The components of this budget are a monthly sales budget, a monthly purchases
        budget, a monthly cash budget, a forecasted income statement for the quarter, and a
        forecasted August 31 balance sheet. The worksheet MASTER has been provided to assist
        you.

        Quest Industries desires to maintain a cash balance of $8,000 at the end of each month.
        If this goal cannot be met, the company borrows the exact amount needed to reach its goal.
        If the company has a cash balance greater than $8,000 and also has loans payable
        outstanding, the amount in excess of $8,000 is paid to the bank. Annual interest of 18% is
        paid on a monthly basis on the outstanding balance.

2.   In the spaces provided below, write the formulas requested on the worksheet. FORMULA1
        has been provided for you as an example.

FORMULA1_____=B10_____		FORMULA12_____
FORMULA2_____		FORMULA13_____
FORMULA3_____		FORMULA14_____
FORMULA4_____		FORMULA15_____
FORMULA5_____		FORMULA16_____
FORMULA6_____		FORMULA17_____
FORMULA7_____		FORMULA18_____
FORMULA8_____		FORMULA19_____
FORMULA9_____		FORMULA20_____
FORMULA10_____		FORMULA21_____
FORMULA11_____		FORMULA22_____

FORMULA23_____   FORMULA26_____

FORMULA24_____   FORMULA27_____

FORMULA25_____   FORMULA28_____

3. Start the spreadsheet program and open the file MASTER from the Student Disk. Enter all the formulas where indicated on the worksheet. Check to be sure that your balance sheet balances. Enter your name in cell A1. Save the completed file as MASTER3. Print the worksheet when done. *Check figures: Forecasted net income (cell D95), $27,957; total assets (cell D105), $324,357.*

4. Review the completed master budget and answer the following questions:

    a. Is Quest Industries expecting to earn a profit during the next quarter? If so, how much?

    b. Does the company need to borrow cash during the quarter? Can it make any repayments? Explain. (Carefully review rows 74 through 80.)

    c. Calculate the debt ratio (total liabilities divided by total assets) for Quest.

WHAT-IF ANALYSIS

5. Suppose the company has to revise its estimates because of a downturn in the economy. Unit sales for July, August, and September will be half (50%) of the original estimates. Revise the estimates in cells B11 through B13. After this is done, check your forecasted balance sheet. It should still balance! What effect will this new state of affairs have on net income, borrowing, and debt ratio? Explain why these items changed.

6. Suppose the company has just the opposite news and now expects unit sales for July, August, and September to be double (200%) the original estimates. What effect will this have on the company's net income, borrowing, and debt ratio? Explain your findings.

143

GRAPHICAL ANALYSIS

7.   Click the Chart sheet tab. You will see a chart plotting sales and net income over a range of sales volumes (100% equals the original problem data). This is a graphical representation of the sales and net income components of requirements 5 and 6. A review of this chart raises two additional questions about the relationship between sales and net income:

      a.   From the chart, estimate sales volumes (roughly), in percentage and dollars, that are required for Quest to break even (net income equals $0) during this quarter.

               Expected volume percent % _____
               Sales (dollars) $_____

      b.   Notice that net income is rising slower than sales volume. Is this a problem?

      When the assignment is complete, close the file without saving it again.

TICKLERS (optional)

Worksheet. Quest wants to have each budget on the MASTER3 worksheet not only show monthly figures but also totals for the quarter. Use column E to present totals for all budget lines (except in the budgeted income statement and balance sheet). Consult your textbook for proper treatment of beginning and ending balances in the production, purchases, and cash budgets. Use the Print Preview command (File menu) to make sure that the worksheet including the totals will print out neatly, then print the worksheet. Save the completed file as MASTERT.

Chart. Using the MASTER3 file, create a 3-D area chart to show the monthly sales volume in units, from April through September. No Chart Data Table is needed; use data from the worksheet. Put your name somewhere on the chart. Save the file again as MASTER3. Print the chart.

	A	B	C	D
2	**MASTER**			
3	*Master Budget*			
4				
5	Data Section			
6				
7	Actual and Budgeted Unit Sales			
8	April	1,500		
9	May	1,000		
10	June	1,600		
11	July	1,400		
12	August	1,500		
13	September	1,200		
14				
15	Balance Sheet, May 31, 2001			
16	Cash	$8,000		
17	Accounts receivable	107,800		
18	Merchandise inventory	52,800		
19	Fixed assets (net)	130,000		
20	Total assets	$298,600		
21				
22	Accounts payable (merchandise)	$74,800		
23	Owner's equity	223,800		
24	Total liabilities & equity	$298,600		
25				
26	Other Data			
27	Average selling price	$98		
28	Average purchase cost per unit	$55		
29	Desired ending inventory			
30	(% of next month's unit sales)	60%		
31	Collections from customers:			
32	Collected in month of sale	20%		
33	Collected in month after sale	60%		
34	Collected two months after sale	20%		
35	Projected cash payments:			
36	Variable expenses	30%	of sales	
37	Fixed expenses (per month)	$10,000		
38	Depreciation per month	$1,000		
39				

	A	B	C	D
40	Answer Section			
41				
42	Sales Budget	June	July	August
43	Units	FORMULA1	0	0
44				
45	Dollars	FORMULA2	0	0
46				
47				
48	Unit Purchases Budget	June	July	August
49	Desired ending inventory	FORMULA3	0	0
50	Current month's unit sales	FORMULA4	0	0
51	Total units needed	FORMULA5	0	0
52	Beginning inventory	FORMULA6	0	0
53	Purchases (units)	FORMULA7	0	0
54				
55	Purchases (dollars)	FORMULA8	$0	$0
56				
57				
58	Cash Budget	June	July	August
59	Cash balance, beginning	$8,000	$0	$0
60	Cash receipts:			
61	Collections from customers:			
62	From April sales	FORMULA9		
63	From May sales	FORMULA10	FORMULA11	
64	From June sales	FORMULA12	0	0
65	From July sales		0	0
66	From August sales			0
67	Total cash available	$0	$0	$0
68	Cash disbursements:			
69	Merchandise	FORMULA13	$0	$0
70	Variable expenses	FORMULA14	0	0
71	Fixed expenses	FORMULA15	0	0
72	Interest paid	0	0	0
73	Total disbursements	$0	$0	$0
74	Cash balance before financing	$0	$0	$0
75	Less: Desired ending balance	0	0	0
76	Excess (deficit) of cash over needs	$0	$0	$0
77	Financing			
78	Borrowing	$0	$0	$0
79	Repayment	0	0	0
80	Total effects of financing	$0	$0	$0
81	Cash balance, ending	$0	$0	$0
82				

	A	B	C	D
83				
84	Forecasted Income Statement			
85	For Quarter Ended August 31, 2001			
86	Sales			FORMULA16
87	Cost of goods sold			FORMULA17
88	Gross profit			FORMULA18
89	Expenses:			
90	Variable expenses			FORMULA19
91	Fixed expenses			FORMULA20
92	Depreciation expense			FORMULA21
93	Interest expense			FORMULA22
94	Total expenses			$0
95	Net income			$0
96				
97				
98	Forecasted Balance Sheet			
99	August 31, 2001			
100	Assets:			
101	Cash			FORMULA23
102	Accounts receivable			FORMULA24
103	Merchandise inventory			FORMULA25
104	Fixed assets (net)			FORMULA26
105	Total assets			$0
106				
107	Liabilities & equity:			
108	Accounts payable			FORMULA27
109	Loans payable			0
110	Owner's equity			FORMULA28
111	Total liabilities & equity			$0
112				

147

P22 ☆ FLEXIBLE BUDGETING (FLEXBUD)

LEARNING OBJECTIVES

- Prepare a flexible budget for overhead costs.
- Interpret differences between static and flexible budget variances.
- Develop budget revisions based on historical results.
- Identify overhead costs by their behavior over increasing volume.
- Alter the worksheet to include an additional overhead cost.
- Create a chart contrasting the budget variances of the static and flexible budgets.

PROBLEM DATA

Sampson Clock Works has just completed an in-depth study of overhead costs. The firm normally operates between 3,600 and 4,600 labor hours each month. Budgeted costs for this range of activity are presented below:

Depreciation	$4,000
Maintenance	$1,800 plus $0.70 per direct labor hour
Indirect labor	$2,800 plus $0.25 per direct labor hour
Utilities	$4,000 plus $0.20 per direct labor hour
Indirect material	$0.25 per direct labor hour
Overtime	$2.25 for each direct labor hour in excess of 4,000 direct labor hours per month

During April, Sampson had planned to operate at 4,500 direct labor hours. Actual activity amounted to only 4,000 hours with the following costs:

Depreciation	$4,000
Maintenance	4,700
Indirect labor	4,240
Utilities	4,850
Indirect material	1,100
Overtime	160

All fixed cost elements remained as budgeted.

REQUIRED

1. The president of the company has asked you to analyze the overhead costs in April by preparing a report making comparisons of actual costs to the original (static) budget which was prepared using the budget data presented above. The vice president of operations is interested in a similar report, but one that utilizes flexible budgeting concepts. The worksheet called FLEXBUD that follows these requirements has been provided for your assistance. Note that the initial problem data is already entered in the Data Section of the worksheet.

2. Using the spaces provided below, enter the 12 formulas required to complete the worksheet. FORMULA6 and FORMULA12 will utilize the =IF function discussed in Appendix A of *Excel Quick*.

    FORMULA1_____   FORMULA7_____

    FORMULA2_____   FORMULA8_____

    FORMULA3_____   FORMULA9_____

    FORMULA4_____   FORMULA10_____

    FORMULA5_____   FORMULA11_____

    FORMULA6_____   FORMULA12_____

3. Start the spreadsheet program and open the file FLEXBUD from the Student Disk. Enter the 12 formulas in the appropriate cells. Enter your name in cell A1. Save your results as FLEXBUD3 and print the worksheet when done. *Check figure: Total flexible budget difference (cell E43), $850 unfavorable.*

4. Comment on the differences between the static and flexible budget performance reports. Which budget is more useful in appraising the performance of the various persons charged with the responsibility for cost control? Why?

WHAT-IF ANALYSIS

5.   The following actual overhead costs were incurred in May:

Depreciation $4,000
Maintenance   5,150
Indirect labor   4,420
Utilities   4,900
Indirect material   1,350
Overtime   1,125

Planned direct labor hours were 4,000. Actual direct labor hours were 4,500. Other budget data for May were identical to April except that fixed maintenance costs have increased to $2,000 and variable indirect materials costs have increased to $0.30 per direct labor hour.

Prepare and print new budget reports for May. Remember to change the month in cell B7. Save your completed file as FLEXBUD5. Compare the two budget reports and comment on the differences disclosed between the static budget and flexible budget performance reports.

6.   If you were to suggest a revision to the budget for May, which cost category seems most in need of revision? Assuming that the fixed cost component of this budgeted cost is already correct, what should the variable cost component be so that the budget equals actual? Try different values in the appropriate cell in the Data Section and write your answer below.

GRAPHICAL ANALYSIS

7.   Click the Chart sheet tab. On the chart, lines are plotting the cost behavior patterns of four of the overhead costs from this problem. Examine the patterns, review the Data Section, and identify below which of the four costs each represents.

A_____
B_____
C_____
D_____

When the assignment is complete, close the file without saving it again.

TICKLERS (optional)

Worksheet. The controller of Sampson Clock Works has discovered that insurance costs were mistakenly omitted from the FLEXBUD3 worksheet. Insert new lines for insurance costs (right under maintenance costs) and redo the April performance reports to include the following information about insurance costs:

Budget: $1,200 per month plus $0.35 per direct labor hour
Actual: $2,500

Use the Print Preview command (File menu) to make sure that the worksheet will print neatly on one page, then print the worksheet. Save the completed file as FLEXBUDT.

Chart. Using the FLEXBUD3 file, prepare a 2-D column chart which graphically represents the budget variances shown on both budgets. No Chart Data Table is needed. Use A28 to A33 as the X-axis. Use E28 to E33 and E37 to E42 as the two data ranges. Use appropriate titles, legends, formats, etc. Put your name somewhere on the chart. Save the file again as FLEXBUD3. Print the chart.

	A	B	C	D	E
2		FLEXBUD			
3		Flexible Budgeting			
4					
5	Data Section				
6					
7	For the month of:	April			
8					
9		Budget Data			
10		Fixed	Variable		Actual
11		Portion	Portion*		Data
12	Depreciation	$4,000	--		$4,000
13	Maintenance	$1,800	$0.70		4,700
14	Indirect labor	$2,800	0.25		4,240
15	Utilities	$4,000	0.20		4,850
16	Indirect material		0.25		1,100
17	Overtime		2.25 **		160
18					
19		*per direct labor hour			
20		**per monthly direct labor hours in excess of			4,000
21					
22		Planned direct labor hours for the month			4,500
23		Actual direct labor hours for the month			4,000
24					
25	Answer Section				
26					
27	Static Budget		Budget	Actual	Difference
28	Depreciation		FORMULA1	$0	$0
29	Maintenance		FORMULA2	0	0
30	Indirect labor		FORMULA3	0	0
31	Utilities		FORMULA4	0	0
32	Indirect material		FORMULA5	0	0
33	Overtime		FORMULA6	0	0
34			$0	$0	$0
35					
36	Flexible Budget		Budget	Actual	Difference
37	Depreciation		FORMULA7	$0	$0
38	Maintenance		FORMULA8	0	0
39	Indirect labor		FORMULA9	0	0
40	Utilities		FORMULA10	0	0
41	Indirect material		FORMULA11	0	0
42	Overtime		FORMULA12	0	0
43			$0	$0	$0
44					

P23 ☼ MATERIAL AND LABOR VARIANCES (PRIMEVAR)

LEARNING OBJECTIVES

- Calculate materials price and quantity variances; calculate labor rate and efficiency variances; automatically label variances as being favorable or unfavorable.
- Interpret cost data to determine proper inputs for variance analysis.
- Interpret variances for management implications.
- Alter the worksheet to include overhead variance analysis (2-, 3-, or 4-way).
- Create a chart comparing standard unit costs with actual unit costs.

PROBLEM DATA

Mark Industries manufactures a product whose standard direct materials and direct labor unit costs are as follows:

Direct materials: 5 pounds at $16 per pound	$80
Direct labor: 6 hours at $8 per hour	48

Actual data for October:
    Actual production: 7,600 units
    Direct materials used in production: 39,500 pounds costing $628,050
    Direct labor: 44,000 hours costing $354,200

REQUIRED

1.   What is the total actual cost of October's production? Based on the standards, what should it have cost? Compute the total difference (variance) between these two amounts.

2.   The president of Mark Industries wants an analysis prepared to help explain why the variance computed in requirement 1 occurred. Using the worksheet called PRIMEVAR that follows these requirements, calculate the material and labor variances for Mark Industries. The problem requires you to enter the input in the Data Section, as well as formulas in the Answer Section.

155

3. Use the problem data above to determine the values (or formulas) to be entered as INPUT A, INPUT B, etc., in the Data Section of the worksheet. For now, pencil them in on the printout of PRIMEVAR.

4. In the spaces provided below, write the formulas requested in the worksheet. FORMULA1 has been done for you as an example. Formulas 8–10 should enter an F if the variance is favorable and a U if it is unfavorable. See the discussion of the =IF function in Appendix A of *Excel Quick*.

FORMULA1_____=(D8-D9)*D12_____   FORMULA6_____

FORMULA2_____   FORMULA7_____

FORMULA3_____   FORMULA8_____

FORMULA4_____   FORMULA9_____

FORMULA5_____   FORMULA10_____

5. Start the spreadsheet program and open the file PRIMEVAR from the Student Disk. Enter the input values or formulas to compute the input values. Then enter the formulas where indicated on the worksheet. Enter your name in cell A1. Save the completed file as PRIMEVA5. Print the worksheet when done. *Check figure: Material quantity variance (cell B27), $24,000 U.*

WHAT-IF ANALYSIS

6. The worksheet you have developed will handle most simple variance analysis problems. Try the problem below for KPW, Inc.:

	Cost Per Unit	
	Standard	Actual
Direct materials:		
Standard: 1.25 pounds at $10 per pound	$12.50	
Actual: 1.20 pounds at $10.50 per pound		$12.60
Direct labor:		
Standard: 3.5 hours at $6.00 per hour	21.00	
Actual: 4 hours at $5.85 per hour		23.40

Actual production for October was 11,500 units. Compute the direct materials and direct labor variances for KPW, Inc. Be careful when entering your input because this problem presents the information in a different format from the Mark Industries' data. Save the file as PRIMEVA6. Print the worksheet when done.

GRAPHICAL ANALYSIS

7. Close the PRIMEVA6 file and open PRIMEVA5. Click the Chart sheet tab. On the screen is a graphical representation of the variances computed in requirement 5. Review the chart and answer the following questions:

    a. Which variances does each bar represent?

        A

        B

        C

        D

    b. Which of the variances shown would be of most concern to management for immediate attention? (Consider groups of variances and materiality also.) Explain.

    When the assignment is complete, close the file without saving it again.

TICKLERS (optional)

Worksheet. Mark Industries also has the following information regarding overhead for October: actual overhead $375,000, standard variable overhead of $3 per direct labor hour, and standard fixed overhead of $5 per direct labor hour (based on 47,000 hours budgeted). Modify the PRIMEVA5 worksheet to compute all appropriate overhead variances. Use the Print Preview command (File menu) to make sure that the worksheet will print neatly on one page, then print the worksheet. Save the completed file as PRIMEVAT.

Hint: Insert several new rows in the Data Section and in the Answer Section.

Chart. Using the PRIMEVA5 file, prepare a 3-D stacked bar chart to compare total standard cost per unit with actual cost per unit. Complete the Chart Tickler Data Table and use it as a basis for preparing the chart. You do not need to use cell references when completing the table. Enter all appropriate titles, legends, and formats. Put your name somewhere on the chart. Save the file again as PRIMEVA5. Print the chart.

	A	B	C	D
2	PRIMEVAR			
3	Material and Labor Variances			
4				
5	Data Section			
6				
7	Materials price variance input			
8	Actual cost of material per pound (ounce, etc.)			INPUT A
9	Standard cost of mat. per pound (ounce, etc.)			INPUT B
10				
11	Materials quantity variance input			
12	Actual quantity of materials used			INPUT C
13	Standard quantity of mat. used for actual output			INPUT D
14				
15	Labor rate variance input			
16	Actual cost of labor per hour			INPUT E
17	Standard cost of labor per hour			INPUT F
18				
19	Labor efficiency variance input			
20	Actual quantity of hours incurred			INPUT G
21	Standard quantity of hours for actual output			INPUT H
22				
23	Answer Section			
24				
25				F or U
26	Material price variance	FORMULA1		FORMULA8
27	Material quantity variance	FORMULA2		FORMULA9
28				
29	Total materials variance		FORMULA3	FORMULA10
30				
31	Labor rate variance	FORMULA4		N/A
32	Labor efficiency variance	FORMULA5		N/A
33				
34	Total labor variance		FORMULA6	N/A
35				
36	Total materials and labor variances		FORMULA7	N/A
37				

P24 ☆ DEPARTMENTAL INCOME STATEMENT (DEPT)

LEARNING OBJECTIVES

- Develop departmental income statements using various cost allocation bases.
- Assess departmental performance using the cost allocation bases.
- Alter the worksheet to determine whether a department should be eliminated; utilize departmental contribution margin and indirect expense analysis.
- Create two charts showing the expense composition of two departments.

PROBLEM DATA

Forked Creek Bungee Supply Inc. has divided its operations into two departments: Supplies, devoted to selling bungee cords and supplies; and Apparel, devoted to selling sports clothing and some bungee wear. Departmental expense accounts are kept for direct expenses, but indirect expenses are not allocated until the end of the accounting period. Selected data at June 30, 2000, the end of the current fiscal year, are as follows:

	Apparel	Supplies	Indirect Expenses
Departmental operating expenses:			
Sales salaries	$18,000	$30,000	
Rent			$19,000
Administrative salaries			25,000
Advertising	3,000	2,000	800
Supplies used	1,175	1,625	
Payroll taxes (12% of salaries)			8,760
Insurance expense			6,400
Depreciation expense	300	350	
Miscellaneous expense	325	220	200
	$22,800	$34,195	$60,160

	Apparel	Supplies	Totals
Other departmental data:			
Net sales	$69,000	$160,000	$229,000
Cost of goods sold	24,000	55,000	79,000
Average inventory	17,000	19,000	36,000
Floor space (square feet)	800	800	1,600
Fixtures (original cost)	2,740	3,260	6,000

The bases for allocating indirect expenses are as follows:

Indirect Expense	Basis of Allocation
Rent	Floor space
Administrative salaries	Gross profit
Advertising	Net sales
Payroll taxes	Direct and indirect salaries
Insurance expense	Sum of fixtures and average inventory
Miscellaneous expense	Supplies used

REQUIRED

1. As the accountant for Forked Creek Bungee Supply, you have been asked to prepare a departmental income statement. Review the worksheet DEPT that follows these requirements. All of the problem information relating to direct expenses has been entered into the Answer Section. You will be allocating the indirect expenses to the appropriate departments.

2. In the spaces provided below, write the formulas requested. FORMULA1 has been provided for you as an example.

FORMULA1____=(B20/D20)*B8_____   FORMULA6_____

FORMULA2_____   FORMULA7_____

FORMULA3_____   FORMULA8_____

FORMULA4_____   FORMULA9_____

FORMULA5_____   FORMULA10_____

3. Start the spreadsheet program and open the file DEPT from the Student Disk. Enter the formulas where indicated on the worksheet. The cells that contain zeros now have been pre-programmed. They will change to non-zero values as the formulas are entered. Enter your name in cell A1. Save your file as DEPT3. Print the worksheet when done. *Check figure: Operating income, Supplies department (cell C47), $34,038.*

4. What conclusions can be drawn from this departmental income statement?

WHAT-IF ANALYSIS

5.   The sales manager for the Apparel department maintains that rent should be allocated on the basis of net sales rather than on floor space. The manager thinks this is fairer since the Supplies department occupies more "prime location" floor space than does the Apparel department. Alter FORMULA1 and FORMULA2 (cells B40 and C40 respectively) on the worksheet to see what effect this "fairer" allocation would have on each department's operating income. Save the revision as DEPT5. Print the worksheet when done.

6.   Comment on the results of this change and on the appropriateness of the new allocation scheme.

GRAPHICAL ANALYSIS

7.   The sales manager of the Apparel department feels she has her direct expenses under control, but she is still concerned with the amount of indirect expenses allocated to her department. She has prepared a chart showing the percentage of sales made by her department and the percentage of expenses incurred. Open DEPT3 and click the Chart sheet tab. Then open DEPT5 and click the Chart sheet tab. Is her concern warranted? Explain.

When the assignment is complete, close the file without saving it again.

TICKLERS (optional)

Worksheet. The president of Forked Creek is considering whether the Apparel department should be eliminated. She wants to see departmental income statements which show each department's contribution toward indirect expenses. Modify the DEPT3 worksheet so that it can help her with this decision. Use the Print Preview command (File menu) to make sure that the worksheet will print neatly on one page, then print the worksheet. Save the revision as DEPTT. Should the Apparel department be eliminated? Explain.

Hint: Insert rows and formulas to subtotal the direct expenses. Use these amounts to determine departmental contribution. Do not allocate the indirect expenses (i.e., erase all allocation formulas and redo the formulas in the total column).

Chart. Using the DEPT3 file, prepare two pie charts, one of which shows the composition of expenses for the Apparel department (cost of goods sold, total direct expenses, and total allocated indirect expenses), and the other for the Supplies department. Complete the Chart Tickler Data Table and use it as a basis for preparing each chart. Enter an appropriate title for each. Put your name somewhere on each chart. Save the file again as DEPT3. Print both charts.

	A	B	C	D
2		**DEPT**		
3		*Departmental Income Statement*		
4				
5	Data Section			
6				
7	Indirect Expenses			
8	Rent	$19,000		
9	Administrative salaries	25,000		
10	Advertising	800		
11	Payroll taxes	8,760		
12	Insurance expense	6,400		
13	Miscellaneous expense	200		
14				
15	Other Departmental Expenses			
16		Apparel	Supplies	Totals
17	Net sales	$69,000	$160,000	$229,000
18	Cost of goods sold	24,000	55,000	79,000
19	Average inventory	17,000	19,000	36,000
20	Floor space (square feet)	800	800	1,600
21	Fixtures (original cost)	2,740	3,260	6,000
22				
23	Answer Section			
24				
25	Forked Creek Bungee Supply Inc.			
26	Departmental Income Statement			
27	June 30, 2000			
28				
29				
30		Apparel	Supplies	Totals
31	Net sales	$69,000	$160,000	$229,000
32	Cost of goods sold	24,000	55,000	79,000
33	Gross profit	$45,000	$105,000	$150,000
34	Operating expenses:			
35	Sales salaries	$18,000	$30,000	$48,000
36	Advertising (direct)	3,000	2,000	5,000
37	Supplies used	1,175	1,625	2,800
38	Depreciation on equipment	300	350	650
39	Miscellaneous expense (direct)	325	220	545
40	Rent	FORMULA1	FORMULA2	FORMULA3
41	Administrative salaries	FORMULA4	FORMULA5	FORMULA6
42	Advertising (indirect)	FORMULA7	0	0
43	Payroll taxes	FORMULA8	0	0
44	Insurance expense	0	FORMULA9	0
45	Miscellaneous expenses (indirect)	0	FORMULA10	0
46	Total operating expenses	$0	$0	$0
47	Operating income	$0	$0	$0
48				

P25 ☼ CAPITAL BUDGETING (CAPBUD)

LEARNING OBJECTIVES

* Evaluate capital investment projects using payback period, accounting rate of return, net present value analysis, and internal rate of return using the =NPV and =IRR functions.
* Perform sensitivity analysis on cost, salvage value, and annual cash flows.
* Interpret investment data to determine proper inputs to capital budgeting decisions.
* Alter the worksheet to include projects with uneven cash flows.
* Create a chart showing the sensitivity of net present value to changes in the cost of the investment.

PROBLEM DATA

The owner of Tons of Tunes, a chain of music and audio mega-stores, is considering renting space in a new shopping mall. It is anticipated that this rental will require an investment in fixtures and equipment costing $190,000, with an estimated salvage value of $10,000 at the end of its useful life in 10 years. The new store is expected to generate annual net cash flow of $40,000. The owner desires a 20% annual return on investment and wants a payback period of less than four years. Ignore the impact of taxes.

REQUIRED

1. Use the worksheet called CAPBUD that follows these requirements to evaluate this investment for the owner. Note that the investment information is already entered in the Data Section of the worksheet. Note also that there is a scratch pad at the bottom of the worksheet. The numbers in the scratch pad are needed as input to the net present value and internal rate of return calculations.

2. In the spaces provided below, enter the four formulas requested. Carefully review Appendix A in *Excel Quick* for instructions on using the =NPV and =IRR functions.

    FORMULA1_____   FORMULA3_____

    FORMULA2_____   FORMULA4_____

3. Start the spreadsheet program and open the file CAPBUD from the Student Disk. Enter the above formulas. Enter your name in cell A1. Save the results as CAPBUD3 and print the worksheet when done. *Check figure: Internal rate of return (cell E18), 16.78%.*

4. Should the owner make the investment in the new store? Explain.

WHAT-IF ANALYSIS

5.   The owner would like to test the sensitivity of the estimates used for the input data to compute the net present value and internal rate of return on this investment. Ignore the payback period and the accounting rate of return. Consider (a), (b), and (c) below independently by holding everything else constant:

   a.   What is the minimum cost of the investment (to the nearest $100) needed for the owner to accept it?

   b.   Reset cost to $190,000. What is the minimum salvage value (to the nearest $100) needed for the owner to accept it?

   c.   Reset salvage value to $10,000. What is the minimum annual cash flow (to the nearest $100) needed for the owner to accept it?

   Comment on the results of these analyses. How sensitive is the decision to accept or reject this investment to the estimates used for input data?

6.   The owner of Tons of Tunes is also considering introducing a laser disc calibration service at another store. The company will have to spend $37,000 for equipment, $3,000 for installation, and $8,000 for testing. The equipment will have no salvage value at the end of four years. Estimated annual results for the project are:

Service fees		$53,000
Expenses other than depreciation	$33,000	
Depreciation (straight-line)	12,000	45,000
Net income		$ 8,000

   Enter the new information in the Data Section. Assuming the owner's criteria for accepting a project have not changed, should Tons of Tunes invest in this service? Explain. Print the worksheet when done.

GRAPHICAL ANALYSIS

7.   Reset the Data Section of the CAPBUD3 worksheet to the original values. In requirement 5, you assessed the sensitivity of the investment's internal rate of return to changes in some of the input data. This was done in a trial-and-error fashion. Click the Chart sheet tab. Presented on the screen is a graphical analysis of the sensitivity of the internal rate of return

to changes in annual cash flows. To demonstrate the usefulness of such a chart, note the ease with which you are able to answer the following questions that might be of interest to the owner:

a. What annual cash flow (approximately) is required to:
 1) Earn 0% rate of return?_____
 2) Earn 20% rate of return?_____
 3) Earn over 30% rate of return?_____
 4) Earn between 10% and 20% rate of return?_____

b. Approximately, how much is the rate of return reduced for each drop of $10,000 annual cash flow?

When the assignment is complete, close the file without saving it again.

TICKLERS (optional)

Worksheet. The CAPBUD3 worksheet handles only cash inflows that are even in amount each year. Many capital projects generate uneven cash inflows. Suppose that the new mega-store had expected cash earnings of $20,000 per year for the first two years, $35,000 for the next four years, and $55,000 for the last four years. The new store will generate the same total cash return ($400,000) as in the original problem, but the timing of the cash flows is different. Alter the CAPBUD3 worksheet so that the NPV and IRR calculations can be made whether there are even or uneven cash flows. When done, use the Print Preview command (File menu) to make sure that the worksheet will print neatly on one page, then print the worksheet. Save the completed file as CAPBUDT.

Hint: One suggestion is to label column F in the scratch pad as Uneven Cash Flows. Enter the uneven cash flows for each year. Modify FORMULA3 to include these cash flows. Modify the formulas in the range E30 to E39 to include the new data. Then set cell E10 (estimated Annual Net Cash Inflow) to zero. When you have even cash flows, use cell E10 and set column F in the scratch pad to zeros. If you have uneven cash flows, set cell E10 to zero and fill in column F in the scratch pad.

Note that this solution causes garbage to come out in cells E15 and E16 because those formulas were not altered. *Check figure for uneven cash flows: NPV cell E17, ($47,226).*

Chart. Using the CAPBUD3 file, develop a chart just like the one used in requirement 7 to show the sensitivity of net present value to changes in cost of the investment amount from $160,000 to $190,000 (use $5,000 increments). Complete the Chart Tickler Data Table and use it as a basis for preparing the chart. Put your name somewhere on the chart. Save the file again as CAPBUD3. Print the chart.

	A	B	C	D	E	F
2	CAPBUD					
3	Capital Budgeting					
4						
5	Data Section					
6						
7	Cost of investment (initial outlay)				$190,000	
8	Estimated life of investment				10	years
9	Estimated salvage value				$10,000	
10	Estimated annual net cash inflow				$40,000	
11	Required rate of return				20.00%	
12						
13	Answer Section					
14						
15	Payback period				FORMULA1	years
16	Accounting (average) rate of return				FORMULA2	
17	Net present value				FORMULA3	
18	Internal rate of return				FORMULA4	
19						
20						
21						
22						
23			Scratch Pad			
24			Cash flow table needed for			
25			NPV & IRR calculations			
26			NPV		IRR	
27			Annual	Salvage	Combined	
28		Year	Cash Flow	Value	Flows	
29		0			-190000	
30		1	40000	0	40000	
31		2	40000	0	40000	
32		3	40000	0	40000	
33		4	40000	0	40000	
34		5	40000	0	40000	
35		6	40000	0	40000	
36		7	40000	0	40000	
37		8	40000	0	40000	
38		9	40000	0	40000	
39		10	40000	10000	50000	
40						

168

MODEL-BUILDING PROBLEM CHECKLIST

Before submitting any model-building solution to your instructor, review the following list to ensure that your worksheet is presented in a clear, concise manner.

1. Enter your name in cell A1 and the name of the file in cell A2. (Use the file name given in the problem.)

2. Include the name of the company, the name of the statement or schedule presented, and the date (e.g., 20X3, 4th Quarter, June). The date should be in an unprotected cell.

3. Use cell references in your formulas wherever possible.

4. Format all cells properly. Place dollar signs ($) at the top of all amount columns and below all subtotal rules.

5. Use zero decimal places whenever decimal accuracy is not required. Generally, if the problem statement does not include cents, your answer will not require cents.

6. Vary column widths to fit the data presented.

7. Place titles at the top of all data columns (one exception is on financial statements where the statement heading is sufficient). Titles should be centered or right justified in the columns.

8. Use Data Sections wherever appropriate. If a Data Section is used, it should be labeled as such.

9. Use file protection where appropriate on the worksheet. Unprotect the cells where changeable data or labels are to be entered.

10. Use upper and lowercase letters as appropriate. Generally uppercase letters are needed as the first letter in all headings and titles.

11. Use the =ROUND function to eliminate rounding discrepancies.

12. Printouts should include no unusual spacing or gaps in the middle of the page. Wide worksheets should be printed using landscape orientation. Use the Size option "Fit all to page" to reduce printouts to a single page if at all possible.

M1 ☼ TRIAL BALANCE

The general ledger of Lemon Bay Consulting shows the following balances at August 31:

Cash	$ 3,010
Accounts receivable	8,775
Prepaid insurance	1,800
Accounts payable	2,850
John Cooper, capital	15,000
John Cooper, drawing	12,000
Consulting fees	25,625
Rent expense	12,000
Salary expense	4,425
Supplies expense	755
Utilities expense	550
Miscellaneous expense	160

Cooper has asked you to develop a worksheet that will serve as a trial balance (file name PTB). Use the data above as input for your model.

Review the Model-Building Problem Checklist on page 169 to ensure that your worksheet is complete. Print the worksheet when done. *Check figure: Total debits, $43,475.*

To test your model, use the following balances at September 30:

Cash	$ 1,805
Accounts receivable	11,810
Prepaid insurance	1,650
Accounts payable	1,495
John Cooper, capital	15,000
John Cooper, drawing	13,500
Consulting fees	32,805
Rent expense	13,800
Salary expense	4,935
Supplies expense	1,010
Utilities expense	605
Miscellaneous expense	185

Print the worksheet when done. *Check figure: Total debits, $49,300.*

CHART (optional)

Using the test data worksheet, prepare a pie chart showing the percentage of each asset to total assets. Print the chart when done.

M2 ✪ FINANCIAL STATEMENTS

The ledger of Mitchell Enterprises showed the following balances after adjustment on June 30, 2000, the end of the current fiscal year:

Accounts payable	$ 75,600	General expenses	$112,350
Accounts receivable	103,890	Interest expense	6,750
Accumulated depreciation—		Merchandise inventory	157,500
equipment	26,250	Prepaid insurance	10,125
S. Mitchell, capital	331,635	Salaries payable	14,700
Cash	80,370	Sales	943,500
Cost of merchandise sold	621,450	Selling expenses	138,750
Equipment	142,500	Withdrawals	18,000

The president of Mitchell has asked you to develop a financial statement worksheet (file name PFS) that includes a single-step income statement, a statement of owner's equity, and a balance sheet. This worksheet will allow the financial statements to be prepared quickly by entering account balances in the appropriate cells on the worksheet. Use the information above as input for your worksheet.

Review the Model-Building Problem Checklist on page 169 to ensure that your worksheet is complete. Print the worksheet when done. *Check figure: Total assets, $468,135.*

To test your model, use the following data for the year ended June 30, 2001:

Accounts payable	$ 67,050	General expenses	$108,150
Accounts receivable	92,700	Interest expense	9,000
Accumulated depreciation—		Merchandise inventory	120,750
equipment	29,400	Prepaid insurance	10,800
S. Mitchell, capital	377,835	Salaries payable	12,450
Cash	74,550	Sales	892,500
Cost of merchandise sold	659,835	Selling expenses	129,450
Equipment	147,000	Withdrawals	27,000

Print the worksheet when done. *Check figure: Total assets, $416,400.*

CHART (optional)

Utilizing the test data worksheet, prepare a pie chart depicting the various expenses (including cost of merchandise sold) incurred by Mitchell Enterprises. Print the chart when done.

M3 ☼ CASH RECEIPTS JOURNAL

The terms of sales on account offered by Gordon's General Store are 2/10, n/30. During the first week of March, the following transactions involved receiving cash:

March 1   Received $793.80 from Seaton Inc. in payment of a February 22 invoice of $810, less discount.
3   Received a loan of $4,500 from First National Bank.
4   Received $558.25 from King World in payment of a February 23 invoice.
5   Received $721.28 from Wagner Corp. in payment of a February 28 invoice of $736, less discount.
7   Cash sales for the week totaled $9,500.

Gordon's General Store has asked you to create a computerized cash receipts journal (file name CRJ). The journal should include one column each for the Date, Account Name, Other Accounts Cr., Sales Cr., Accounts Receivable Cr., Sales Discount Dr., and Cash Dr. The appropriate columns should be totaled. Use the data for the first week in March as input for the worksheet.

Review the Model-Building Problem Checklist on page 169 to ensure that your worksheet is complete. Print the worksheet when done. *Check figure: Total debits, $16,104.25.*

To test your model, use the following information for the second week of March:

March 8   Received $426.30 from XYZ Inc. in payment of a March 1 invoice of $435, less discount.
9   Received $896.70 from King World in payment of a February 28 invoice of $915, less discount.
12   Received $712.75 from Ives Stores in payment of a March 1 invoice.
13   Received $150 for old store equipment that had no book value.
14   Cash sales for the week totaled $9,000.

Print the worksheet when done. *Check figure: Total debits, $11,212.75.*

CHART (optional)

Using your test model, create a 3-D column chart showing the amount of cash Gordon's General Store collected from each customer the second week of March. Print the chart when done.

172

M4 ✧ DISCOUNTED NOTES RECEIVABLE

Vora Enterprises holds a 60-day, 8% note for $20,000, dated August 1, that was received from a customer on account. On September 3, the note is discounted at First National Bank at the rate of 11%.

Develop a worksheet (file name NOTEDISC) that can be used to calculate the cash proceeds from the note when it is discounted. Use the above numbers given by Vora Enterprises as sample data for your model.

Review the Model-Building Problem Checklist on page 169 to ensure that your model is complete. Print the worksheet when done. *Check figure: Cash proceeds, $20,098.*

Use the following data from another note that Vora Enterprises holds to test your model. This 90-day, 10% note for $10,000, dated June 2, was received from another customer on account. On June 17, the note is discounted at First National Bank at the rate of 13%.

Print the worksheet when done. *Check figure: Cash proceeds, $9,973.*

CHART (optional)

Using the test data, prepare a line chart which compares the face value of the note to the cash proceeds of the note after discounting. Use as your X-axis the discounting periods of 15, 30, 45, 60, 75, and 90 days. Print the chart when done.

M5 ✿ RETAIL METHOD OF INVENTORY COSTING

Selected data on merchandise inventory, purchases, and sales for Eagle Enterprises for the month of October are as follows:

	Cost	Retail
Merchandise inventory, October 1	$158,850	$299,100
Purchases	94,800	180,900
Purchases returns and allowances	1,650	—
Sales		189,900
Sales returns and allowances		5,250

Develop a worksheet that uses the retail method to automatically compute an estimate of ending inventory (file name RETAIL). The flexibility of your worksheet could be greatly enhanced by using a Data Section. Use the October data above as input for your worksheet.

Review the Model-Building Problem Checklist on page 169 to ensure that your worksheet is complete. Print the worksheet when done. *Check figure: Ending inventory at approximate cost, $155,059.*

To test your model, use the following data for November:

	Cost	Retail
Merchandise inventory, November 1	$155,059	$295,350
Purchases	90,750	208,200
Purchases returns and allowances	2,550	—
Sales		300,000
Sales returns and allowances		6,000

Print the worksheet when done. *Check figure: Ending inventory at approximate cost, $101,231.*

CHART (optional)

Design a 3-D column chart that depicts merchandise available for sale at cost and at retail for both October and November. Print the chart when done.

M6 ☼ INVENTORY VALUATION: LOWER OF COST OR MARKET

Information about Land of Sleep's inventory at June 30, is as follows:

Mattress	Inventory Quantity	Unit Cost	Unit Market
Queen	75	$240	$235
King	165	310	330
Double	43	150	155
Twin	120	105	90

You have been asked to develop a worksheet that will determine the value of the inventory on an item-by-item basis at the lower of cost or market value (file name LCOM). You should find it helpful to use the =MIN function discussed in Appendix A of *Excel Quick*. Use the data above as input for your worksheet.

Review the Model-Building Problem Checklist on page 169 to ensure that your worksheet is complete. Print the worksheet when done. *Check figure: Lower of cost or market inventory value, $86,025.*

To test your model, use the following information about Land of Sleep's inventory at September 30:

Mattress	Inventory Quantity	Unit Cost	Unit Market
Queen	90	$240	$245
King	145	310	315
Double	45	150	145
Twin	160	105	100

Print the worksheet when done. *Check figure: Lower of cost or market inventory value, $89,075.*

CHART (optional)

From the test data worksheet, design a 3-D column chart demonstrating the relationship between total cost and total market value for each commodity. Print the chart when done.

M7 ☼ PLANT ASSET RECORD

Information about one of Power Manufacturing's plant assets—a forklift—is as follows:

Cost	$17,500
Estimated residual value	2,500
Depreciation method	Straight-line
Date purchased	9/01/X1
Estimated life	10 years

The company has hired you to develop a computerized subsidiary ledger form for plant assets (file name PAR). A separate ledger account is to be maintained for each asset. Your form should contain basic facts about the asset (such as date purchased, etc.), depreciation charged each period, accumulated depreciation to date, and book value. The model you develop should automatically update the accumulated depreciation and the book value of the asset after each entry. Record the acquisition of the machine and depreciation for the first three years. Assume that the firm's annual accounting cycle ends on December 31.

Review the Model-Building Problem Checklist on page 169 to ensure that your worksheet is complete. Print the worksheet when done. *Check figure: Book value of forklift, $14,000.*

To test your model, use the following information for a snowplow:

Cost	$6,000
Estimated residual value	150
Depreciation method	Double-declining balance
Date purchased	1/01/X1
Estimated life	12 years

Print the worksheet when done. *Check figure: Book value of snowplow, $3,472.*

CHART (optional)

Using the test data, prepare a line chart showing the book value of the snowplow from date of purchase to 12/31/X3. Print the chart when done.

M8 ☆ PERCENTAGE OF CONTRACT COMPLETION

In 2000, South Square Contracting was working on several contracts. Relevant information about one of the projects is as follows:

Contract A: Total contract price $6,200,000
               Total anticipated costs   4,300,145
               Costs incurred during current year   367,214

South Square Contracting realizes the revenue from construction contracts by the percentage-of-contract-completion method. The company measures percentage-of-contract-completion by the ratio of current period construction costs to total anticipated construction costs. South Square has hired you to develop a worksheet (file name PERCOM) that will quickly and accurately compute current year profit on any of its contracts at any time. Your worksheet should include a Data Section. Use the information for Contract A as input for your model.

Review the Model-Building Problem Checklist on page 169 to ensure that your worksheet is complete. Print the worksheet when done. *Check figure: Current year profit from Contract A, $162,239.*

To test your model, use the following information for Contract B:

Contract B: Total contract price $4,600,500
               Total anticipated costs   2,170,560
               Costs incurred during current year   1,487,495

Print the worksheet when done. *Check figure: Current year profit from Contract B, $1,665,249.*

CHART (optional)

Prepare a 3-D stacked column chart showing how total contract price is broken down between total anticipated costs and total anticipated profits for both Contracts A and B. Print the chart when done.

M9 ☆ PARTNERSHIP: DIVISION OF NET INCOME

J. Ashby and K. Malone recently formed a partnership. Ashby invested $30,000 cash, and Malone invested $30,000 of plant assets and $15,000 cash. The partners are trying to find an equitable way of splitting the income to take into account that Malone invested more capital, but Ashby will spend twice as much time as Malone in running the business. They have asked you to develop a worksheet (file name PSHIP) to allow them to see the effect of:

- Various interest rates on invested capital
- Various salary allowances for time spent
- Various levels of partnership net income

The easiest way to achieve this flexibility is to use a Data Section. Use the following information as input for your model:

Net income	$75,000
Division of net income:	
Interest on original investments at 15%	
Salary allowances:	
Ashby	60,000
Malone	30,000
Remainder shared equally	

Review the Model-Building Problem Checklist on page 169 to ensure that your worksheet is complete. Print the worksheet when done. *Check figure: Ashby net income, $50,625.*

To test your model, use the following profit-sharing scenario:

Net income	$125,000
Division of net income:	
Interest on original investments at 15%	
Salary allowances:	
Ashby	50,000
Malone	25,000
Remainder shared equally	

Print the worksheet when done. *Check figure: Ashby net income, $73,875.*

CHART (optional)

Using the test data provided, prepare a 3-D stacked column chart showing the division of net income (salary, interest, and remainder) to each partner. Print the chart when done.

M10 ✿ INCOME STATEMENT

The following data were selected from the records of Magnuson Incorporated for the month ended April 30:

Advertising expense	$10,100	Insurance expense	$ 500
Depreciation expense—		Interest expense	2,500
office equipment	500	Loss from disposal of a	
Depreciation expense—store		segment of business	23,000
equipment	2,500	Merchandise inventory, April 1	75,000
Extraordinary loss	10,000	Merchandise inventory, April 30	68,000
Income tax:		Office salaries expense	17,000
On continuing operations	15,000	Office supplies expense	1,025
Reduction applicable to loss		Purchases	300,000
from disposal of a segment		Rent expense	500
of the business	4,500	Sales	452,500
Reduction applicable to		Sales salaries expense	15,000
extraordinary loss	1,100	Store supplies expense	2,525

This firm's accounting system generates these totals on a monthly basis. You have been asked to develop a worksheet (file name IS) that will allow a monthly income statement to be prepared by entering monthly figures in the appropriate cells. The income statement should include a section for earnings per share. There were 20,000 shares of common stock (no preferred) outstanding throughout the month. Use the data above as input for your worksheet.

Review the Model-Building Problem Checklist on page 169 to ensure that your worksheet is complete. Print the worksheet when done. *Check figure: April net income, $50,950.*

To test your model, use the following data for the month ended May 31:

Advertising expense	$11,500	Insurance expense	$ 500
Depreciation expense—		Interest expense	6,000
office equipment	810	Loss from disposal of a segment	
Depreciation expense—		of business (additional ex-	
store equipment	3,235	penses from April disposal)	1,000
Extraordinary loss (additional		Merchandise inventory, May 1	68,000
expenses from April loss)	7,500	Merchandise inventory, May 31	70,000
Income tax:		Office salaries expense	20,000
On continuing operations	10,000	Office supplies expense	935
Reduction applicable to loss		Purchases	251,200
from disposal of a segment		Rent expense	1,000
of the business	400	Sales	350,000
Reduction applicable to		Sales salaries expense	26,250
extraordinary loss	1,600	Store supplies expense	3,150

There was no change in the number of shares of common stock outstanding. Print the worksheet when done. *Check figure: May net income, $10,920.*

CHART (optional)

From the test data worksheet, develop a pie chart that presents the percentage distribution of selling expenses. Print the chart when done.

M11 ☆ BOOK VALUE PER SHARE

A prospective investor has hired you to develop a worksheet that will compute the book value per share (file name BVALUE) on each class of stock of various companies. Your worksheet should include a Data Section.

One of the companies the investor is currently interested in is Pelican Enterprises which has the following capital structure:

Preferred 14% stock, $35 par	$1,575,000
Premium on preferred stock	96,000
Common stock, $30 par	2,025,000
Premium on common stock	123,000
Retained earnings	525,000

Preferred stock has a prior claim to assets on liquidation to the extent of 120% of par.

Review the Model-Building Problem Checklist on page 169 to ensure that your worksheet is complete.   Print the worksheet when done.   *Check figure: Book value per share, Pelican Enterprises: Common, $36.36.*

To test your model, use the following data for Osprey Corporation:

Preferred 12% stock, $45 par	$1,350,000
Premium on preferred stock	127,500
Common stock, $25 par	1,875,000
Premium on common stock	135,000
Retained earnings	487,500

Preferred stock has a prior claim to assets on liquidation to the extent of 110% of par.

Print the worksheet when done. *Check figure: Book value per share, Osprey Corporation: Common, $33.20.*

CHART (optional)

Using the test worksheet, prepare a pie chart that shows how much of the total equity is allocated to preferred stock and how much is allocated to common stock. Print the chart when done.

M12 ✡ CONSTANT DOLLAR INCOME STATEMENT

The following income statement was prepared from the records of Manasota Corporation at December 31, the end of the current fiscal year:

Manasota Corporation
Income Statement
For Year Ended December 31, 2000

Revenue		$165,000
Expenses:		
Depreciation expense on equipment	$24,000	
Rent expense	15,000	
Supplies expense	4,500	
Wages expense	84,000	
Miscellaneous expense	1,350	128,850
Net income		$ 36,150

Revenue, miscellaneous expense, rent expense, and wages expense occurred evenly throughout the year. Equipment was acquired when the price index was 140, and supplies were acquired when the price index was 163. The price index averaged 156 for the year and was 164 at the end of the year. Develop a worksheet (file name CDOLLAR) to translate Manasota's historical cost income statement into a constant dollar income statement. Your worksheet should include a Data Section. Use the data above as input for your model. The purchasing power loss on monetary items was $8,000.

Review the Model-Building Problem Checklist on page 169 to ensure that your worksheet is complete. Print the worksheet when done. *Check figure: Constant dollar net income, $27,324.*

To test your model, use the information below for the following year:

Manasota Corporation
Income Statement
For Year Ended December 31, 2001

Revenue		$180,000
Expenses:		
Depreciation expense on equipment	$24,000	
Rent expense	20,000	
Supplies expense	3,000	
Wages expense	94,000	
Miscellaneous expense	1,200	142,200
Net income		$ 37,800

Revenue, miscellaneous expense, rent expense, and wages expense occurred evenly throughout the year. Equipment was acquired when the price index was 140, and supplies were acquired when the price index was 165. The price index averaged 166 for the year and was 168 at the end of the year. The purchasing power loss on monetary items was $7,500.

Print the worksheet when done. *Check figure: Constant dollar net income, $26,226.*

CHART (optional)

Utilizing the test data, create a pie chart showing the proportionate breakdown of total restated expenses for the year. Print the chart when done.

M13 ☆ DEFERRED INCOME TAX

Differences in accounting methods between those applied to its accounts and those used in determining taxable income yielded the following amounts for the first three years of Durango Tool and Die:

	First Year	Second Year	Third Year
Income before income tax	$563,000	$614,000	$647,000
Taxable income	539,000	623,000	630,000

The income tax rate for each of the three years was 40% of taxable income, and taxes were paid promptly each year. The president of Durango has asked you to develop a worksheet (file name DEFERTAX) that will show income tax deducted on the income statement, income tax payments for the year, year's addition to (deduction from) deferred income tax payable, and the year-end balance of deferred income tax payable. Use the information above as input for the Data Section of your worksheet.

Review the Model-Building Problem Checklist on page 169 to ensure that your worksheet is complete. Print the worksheet when done. *Check figure: Durango Tool and Die, year-end balance of deferred tax payable, third year, $12,800.*

The president of Consolidated Enterprises is impressed with your model and wishes to test it using the following data from Consolidated (assume a 40% tax rate):

	First Year	Second Year	Third Year
Income before income tax	$657,000	$652,000	$713,000
Taxable income	627,000	660,000	675,000

Print the worksheet when done. *Check figure: Consolidated Enterprises year-end balance of deferred tax payable, third year, $24,000.*

CHART (optional)

Using the Consolidated Enterprises data, create a 3-D column chart showing the annual addition to or reduction in deferred taxes for all three years. Print the chart when done.

M14 ☆ TAXABLE INCOME (MARRIED, FILING JOINTLY)

Joanna and Jim Johnson have one child and have contributed more than half of the cost of supporting Joanna's mother, who received gross income of $1,200 during the year. During the current year ended December 31, Jim realized a net long-term capital gain of $5,400. Other details of receipts and disbursements during the year are as follows:

Joanna's gross salary	$48,000	Rental property:	
Jim's gross salary	37,000	Real estate tax	$ 2,500
Dividends on corporation		Insurance	750
stock	600	Depreciation	1,850
Rent from property owned	12,000	Interest on mortgage	2,300
Interest on municipal bonds	850	Real estate tax on	
Safe deposit box rental	150	residence	5,500
State sales tax on items		Mortgage interest on	
purchased for personal use	850	residence	11,000
Automobile license fees	75	Charge account interest	600
Charitable contributions	2,600	City income taxes	400
Tax preparation fee	400	State income taxes	4,600
		Medical bills	1,500

You have been hired by a local CPA firm to design a worksheet that will calculate taxable income for married couples filing joint returns (file name MFJTAX). Do not use a Data Section. Set up the worksheet in a standard tax return format. Use the above data as input for your model.

Review the Model-Building Problem Checklist on page 169 to ensure that your worksheet is complete. Print the worksheet when done. *No check figure is provided because tax rules change each year.*

To test your model, use the following information about Debbie and Dave Ducharme, who have three children and incurred a net long-term capital gain of $8,500:

Debbie's gross salary	$13,000	Rental property:	
Dave's gross salary	30,000	Real estate tax	$3,000
Dividends on corporation		Insurance	990
stock	800	Depreciation	2,100
Rent from property owned	14,000	Interest on mortgage	3,000
Interest on municipal bonds	600	Real estate tax on	
Safe deposit box rental	50	residence	1,800
State sales tax on items		Mortgage interest on	
purchased for personal use	800	residence	4,100
Automobile license fees	100	Charge account interest	600
Charitable contributions	1,500	City income taxes	300
Tax preparation fee	300	State income taxes	2,300
		Medical bills	5,250

Print the worksheet when done. *No check figure is provided because tax rules change each year.*

CHART (optional)

Using the data from the test model, create a pie chart showing the proportionate amount of the various taxes claimed as itemized deductions by the Ducharmes. Print the chart when done.

M15 ☼ BOND PREMIUM AND DISCOUNT AMORTIZATION SCHEDULE

On July 1, Bishop Company issued $800,000 of 10-year, 14% bonds at an effective interest rate of 13%. This netted the company $843,410. Interest on the bonds is payable annually on July 1. The president of Bishop has asked you to develop an amortization schedule worksheet (file name AMORT) that will use the effective interest method to calculate annual interest expense, premium (or discount) amortization, unamortized premium (or discount), and bond carrying amount. Your worksheet should include a Data Section.

Review the Model-Building Problem Checklist on page 169 to ensure that your worksheet is complete. Print the worksheet when done. *Check figure: Amortization of bond premium in year 10, $7,080.*

To test your model, calculate the annual interest expense, discount amortization, unamortized discount, and bond carrying amount of $600,000 of 10-year, 8% bonds at an effective interest rate of 9%. The issuance of these bonds netted the company $561,494. Interest on the bonds is payable annually. Print the worksheet when done. *Check figure: Amortization of bond discount in year 10, $5,505.*

CHART (optional)

With information from the test data, create a 3-D area chart that shows annual interest paid and interest expense over the 10-year life of the bond. Print the chart when done.

M16 ☆ VERTICAL ANALYSIS

Liz Prince manages several properties for real estate investors. Each month she reviews the cash flow statements from each property to look for trouble spots. Information for one of the properties, Crossroads Apartments, is as follows:

Crossroads
Statement of Cash Receipts and Expenses

Revenue:		
Rental revenue		$750,000
Vending machine revenue		7,500
Total revenue		$757,500
Expenses:		
Advertising expense	$ 8,000	
Administrative expense	44,100	
Utilities expense	60,000	
Maintenance and repairs expense	54,500	
Real estate tax expense	88,200	
Insurance expense	6,000	
Interest expense	309,000	
Total expenses		569,800
Net cash flow		$187,700

Liz has asked you to develop a worksheet that will automatically prepare a vertical analysis of the cash flow data (file name VERT). All percentages should be based on total revenue. Use the data above as input for your model.

Review the Model-Building Problem Checklist on page 169 to ensure that your worksheet is complete. Print the worksheet when done. *Check figure: Crossroads interest expense is 41% of total revenue.*

To test your model, use the following information for MacLean Manor.

MacLean Manor
Statement of Cash Receipts and Expenses

Revenue:

Rental revenue		$135,000
Vending machine revenue		9,930
Total revenue		$144,930

Expenses:

Advertising expense	$ 3,330	
Administrative expense	5,075	
Utilities expense	8,475	
Maintenance and repairs expense	3,375	
Real estate tax expense	12,000	
Insurance expense	3,330	
Interest expense	30,000	
Total expenses		65,585
Net cash flow		$ 79,345

Print the worksheet when done. *Check figure: MacLean Manor interest expense is 21% of total revenue.*

CHART (optional)

Using the test data worksheet, prepare a pie chart of the expenses. Use short titles for the X-axis. Print the chart when done.

M17 ✪ JOB ORDER COST SHEET

At the present time, Tapper Technology is preparing a bid for a contract to produce 3,000 Siesta flanges. The deadline for bids is December 31, 2000. The predicted costs of production are as follows:

Dept.	Direct Material Amount	Direct Labor Hourly Rate	Hours
Assembly	$1,200	$14.00	150
Painting	7,500	15.00	450
Packaging	1,530	7.00	75

The president has asked you to develop a computerized job order cost sheet (file name JOBSHEET) that can be used to determine the company's bid on a particular contract. Factory overhead is applied at the rate of 70% of direct labor cost, and Tapper uses a 40% markup rate on total manufacturing cost in determining its bid prices. The cost sheet that you develop should include a heading with a description of the job and the deadline date for bidding. The worksheet should be formatted to express all values except labor rates as integers. Use the data above as input for your worksheet.

Review the Model-Building Problem Checklist on page 169 to ensure that your worksheet is complete. Print the worksheet when done. *Check figure: Bid price on Siesta flanges, $36,635.*

To test your model, use the following data which pertains to a prospective contract to produce 15,000 Siesta subassemblies (deadline for bids is January 31, 2001):

Dept.	Direct Material Amount	Direct Labor Hourly Rate	Hours
Assembly	$3,300	$14.50	150
Painting	1,350	16.00	450
Packaging	750	9.75	75

Print the worksheet when done. *Check figure: Bid price on Siesta subassemblies, $38,084.*

CHART (optional)

Using your test model, design a pie chart that shows the proportionate amount of direct materials that each department uses. Print the chart when done.

M18 ☆ HIGH-LOW POINTS METHOD

An examination of monthly production and cost data over a period of several months for Industrial Edge reveals that the highest and lowest levels of production are as follows:

	Total Units Produced	Total Costs
Highest level	180,000	$423,000
Lowest level	75,000	255,000

It is estimated that 135,000 units will be produced next month. Develop a worksheet (file name HL) that can be used to calculate variable cost per unit and total fixed cost using the high-low points method. Then use the estimate to calculate the estimated cost of producing next month's output.

Review the Model-Building Problem Checklist on page 169 to ensure that your worksheet is complete. Print the worksheet when done. *Check figure: Estimated variable cost per unit for Industrial Edge, $1.60.*

To test your model, use the following information from Danforth Inc.:

	Total Units Produced	Total Costs
Highest level	3,300	$44,300
Lowest level	1,800	33,500

Estimate the cost of producing 3,200 units. Print the worksheet when done. *Check figure: Estimated variable cost per unit for Danforth Inc., $7.20.*

CHART (optional)

From the test data worksheet, create an XY chart plotting the high and low points. Use units produced as the X-axis (X-axis range) and total costs as the Y-axis (Series 1). Print the chart when done.

M19 ☆ COST-VOLUME-PROFIT ANALYSIS

In 2000, Sorrento Enterprises anticipates fixed costs of $300,000. Variable costs and expenses are expected to be 60% of sales. The president has asked you to develop a worksheet to calculate sales needed to break even and sales needed to achieve any desired net income (file name DESNI). Your worksheet should include a Data Section that contains fixed costs, desired net income, and variable costs as a percentage of sales. Assume as initial input for your model that the company wishes to achieve a net income of $75,000.

Review the Model-Building Problem Checklist on page 169 to ensure that your worksheet is complete. Print the worksheet when done. *Check figure: Sales needed for desired net income, $937,500.*

To test your model, use the following projections for 2001: fixed costs of $375,000 and variable costs and expenses to equal 40% of sales. The company wishes to have a net income of $90,000. Print the worksheet when done. *Check figure: Sales needed for desired net income, $775,000.*

CHART (optional)

Using the test data worksheet, develop a standard break-even line chart that plots total revenue and total costs from a sales level of $0 to $900,000. Use $100,000 increments on the X-axis.

M20 ☆ GROSS PROFIT ANALYSIS

Beacon Hill Incorporated manufactures several products. In December of 2000, the board of directors decided to raise the price of Product X from $60, which had prevailed throughout 2000, to $66, effective January 1, 2001. The comparative gross profits for Product X for 2000 and 2001 are as follows:

	2001	2000
Sales of Product X	$325,000	$328,000
Cost of goods sold	180,000	195,000
Gross profit	$145,000	$133,000

The board is pleased with the increase in gross profit but would like to know what effect each of the following factors had on causing the increase:

- Increase in selling price
- Increase (if any) in unit sales volume
- Decrease (if any) in unit costs

The president of Beacon Hill Incorporated has asked you to develop a computerized gross profit analysis report (file name GPANAL). Your worksheet should include a Data Section that contains sales, cost of goods sold, gross profit, and unit sales price for each year, as well as the change from one year to another for each. The worksheet should also compute unit costs for each year and the number of units sold.

Review the Model-Building Problem Checklist on page 169 to ensure that your worksheet is complete. Print the worksheet when done. *Check figure: Reduction of sales of Product X attributed to decrease in quantity sold, $32,545.*

To test your model, use the following information for Product Y which sold for $40 in 2000 and $42 in 2001:

	2001	2000
Sales of Product Y	$900,000	$750,000
Cost of goods sold	475,000	450,000
Gross profit	$425,000	$300,000

Print the worksheet when done. *Check figure: Increase in sales of Product Y attributed to increase in quantity sold, $107,143.*

CHART (optional)

Using the test model worksheet, design a 3-D column chart showing how the dollar amount of each of the four variances contributed to the change in gross profit. Print the chart when done.

M21 ☆ CASH BUDGETING

Puss & Pup Pet Store is concerned about its cash position at the end of November because of the anticipated inventory buildup during that month to get ready for the holiday season. Selected information about expected November activity is presented below:

Cash balance, November 1, 2001	$14,000
Sales	$210,000
Gross profit percent (based on sales)	45%
Decrease in accounts receivable during month	$12,000
Increase in accounts payable during month	$51,000
Increase in inventory during month	$90,000

Selling expenses total $32,000 per month plus 15% of sales. Depreciation expense of $5,000 per month is included in fixed selling expenses.

Prepare a worksheet (file name CASHBGT) which will allow Puss & Pup to compute its projected cash balance at the end of November. Your worksheet should include a Data Section and it should be designed so that it could be reused any month.

Review the Model-Building Problem Checklist on page 169 to ensure that your worksheet is complete. Print the worksheet when done. *Check figure: Projected ending cash balance, $23,000.*

To test your model, use the following estimates for December:

Cash balance, December 1, 2001	$23,000
Sales	$270,000
Gross profit percent (based on sales)	40%
Increase in accounts receivable during month	$30,000
Increase in accounts payable during month	$15,000
Decrease in inventory during month	$36,000

Selling expenses total $39,000 per month plus 14% of sales. Depreciation expense of $6,000 per month is included in fixed selling expenses. Print the worksheet when done. *Check figure: Projected ending cash balance, $81,200.*

CHART (optional)

Using the test worksheet, prepare a 3-D column chart showing the effects that sales, cost of goods sold, change in accounts receivable, change in accounts payable, and change in inventory have on the projected ending cash balance. Print the chart when done.

M22 ☼ SALES AND PRODUCTION BUDGETS

The Fudge Factory produces two kinds of fudge—chocolate and peanut butter. Estimated production and sales data for April are as follows:

	Chocolate	Peanut Butter
Beginning inventory (units), April 1	45,000	30,000
Desired inventory (units), April 30	30,000	60,000
Expected sales volume (units):		
North side store	21,000	36,000
South side store	15,000	30,000
Unit sales price	$7.50	$6.70

You have been asked to prepare a computerized sales budget (units and dollars) and a production budget (file name SPBUD). Use the data above as input for your model.

Review the Model-Building Problem Checklist on page 169 to ensure that your worksheet is complete. Print the worksheet when done. *Check figure: Peanut butter fudge production, 96,000 units.*

To test your model, use the following estimates for May:

	Chocolate	Peanut Butter
Beginning inventory (units), May 1	18,000	45,000
Desired inventory (units), May 31	14,000	60,000
Expected sales volume (units):		
North side store	21,000	45,000
South side store	23,000	36,000
Unit sales price	$7.80	$7.00

Print the worksheet when done. *Check figure: Peanut butter fudge production, 96,000 units.*

CHART (optional)

Using the test model, prepare a pie chart depicting the percentage of dollar sales of chocolate fudge at the north side store as compared to the south side store. Print the chart when done.

M23 ✿ VARIANCE ANALYSIS

Hook Manufacturing makes dashboards for cars. During June, 40,000 dashboards were manufactured with standard costs and actual costs for direct materials, direct labor, and factory overhead as follows:

	Standard Costs	**Actual Costs**
Direct materials	10,000 pounds $9	10,600 pounds $10.50
Direct labor	20,000 hours $13	20,600 hours $12.50
Factory overhead	Rates per direct labor hour, based on normal capacity of 30,000 labor hours:	
	Variable cost $5.00	Variable cost $84,000
	Fixed cost $3.75	Fixed cost $49,000

You have been asked to develop a worksheet that will calculate the quantity variance, price variance, total direct materials cost variance, time variance, rate variance, total direct labor cost variance, volume variance, controllable variance, and total factory overhead cost variance (file name VARIANCE). Use the information above as input for the Data Section of your worksheet.

Review the Model-Building Problem Checklist on page 169 to ensure that your worksheet is complete. Print the worksheet when done. *Check figure: Factory overhead volume variance, $37,500 U.*

To test your model, use the following information for the manufacture of 60,000 dashboards during July:

	Standard Costs	**Actual Costs**
Direct materials	16,000 pounds $11	14,800 pounds $11.75
Direct labor	30,000 hours $15	28,400 hours $16.25
Factory overhead	Rates per direct labor hour, based on normal capacity of 30,000 labor hours:	
	Variable cost $5.00	Variable cost $133,000
	Fixed cost $3.75	Fixed cost $98,000

Print the worksheet when done. *Check figure: Factory overhead volume variance, $0.*

CHART (optional)

Using the test model worksheet, create a 3-D column chart that plots the four materials and labor variances (quantity, price, time, and rate). Print the chart when done.

M24 ☼ INCREMENTAL ANALYSIS—
EQUIPMENT REPLACEMENT DECISION

Barbara's Bakery is considering the replacement of an oven that the company has used for three years. Relevant data about the old and new ovens are as follows:

Old Oven:

Cost (10-year life when purchased)	$ 7,000
Annual depreciation	700
Annual operating costs	10,000
Estimated current selling price	4,400

New Oven:

Cost (7-year life)	$14,700
Annual depreciation	2,100
Estimated annual operating costs	8,000

Annual revenue is not expected to change if the new oven is purchased. You have been asked to develop a worksheet that will calculate the net cost reduction or net cost increase associated with purchasing the new oven (file name SUNK). Your analysis should include all seven years. Assume no residual value at the end of seven years for either machine. Some of the above data may be irrelevant to the replacement decision and need not be included in your model. Use the information above as input for the Data Section of your worksheet.

Review the Model-Building Problem Checklist on page 169 to ensure that your worksheet is complete. Print the worksheet when done. *Check figure: Net cost reduction for new oven, $3,700.*

To test your model, use the following data. Barbara's Bakery is considering replacing a dishwasher which it has been using for two years. Assume no residual value at the end of three years for either dishwasher.

Old Dishwasher:

Cost (5-year life when purchased)	$3,800
Annual depreciation	760
Annual operating costs	5,600
Estimated current selling price	2,100

New Dishwasher:

Cost (3-year life)	$4,200
Annual depreciation	1,400
Estimated annual operating costs	5,200

Print the worksheet when done. *Check figure: Net cost increase for new dishwasher, $900.*

CHART (optional)

Making use of the test data, prepare a 3-D column chart that shows the annual operating costs of both dishwashers. Print the chart when done.

M25 ☼ INSTALLMENT SALES

During the month of June, Jasper Furniture Emporium received the following amounts in payment of sales that took place in 1999, 2000, and 2001:

Year of Sale	Amount Received this Month
1999	$15,300
2000	19,740
2001	8,200

Jasper uses the installment method of accounting and recognizes gross profit based on the following historical rates:

33% for 1999 sales
30% for 2000 sales
27% for 2001 sales

You are to develop a worksheet (file name INSTALL) that will calculate the amount of net income recognized in June under the installment method described above. Assume that operating expenses for the month total $10,400.

Review the Model-Building Problem Checklist on page 169 to ensure that your worksheet is complete. Print the worksheet when done. *Check figure: Net income realized, $2,785*

To test your model, use the following receipts for July, when operating expenses totaled $9,900:

Year of Sale	Amount Received this Month
1999	$16,040
2000	17,460
2001	10,920

Print the worksheet when done. *Check figure: Net income realized, $3,580.*

CHART (optional)

Using the test data, design a 3-D column chart that shows amount received this month compared to gross profit recognized. Do this for all three years. Print the chart when done.

C1 ☆ FINANCIAL STATEMENT PREPARATION

Goodness Sakes Inc., a chain of stores selling religious merchandise, has provided you with the following list of accounts and balances for the year ended June 30, 2000. All amounts shown are in thousands of dollars. You have been asked by the company's chief financial officer (CFO) to use a spreadsheet to prepare financial statements for Goodness, including an income statement, a statement of retained earnings, a classified balance sheet, and (if required by your instructor) a statement of cash flows. The CFO can't remember the accounts receivable balance. She asks you to figure it out when you prepare the balance sheet.

The financial information presented below is accumulated in a file named FINANCL on your Student Disk. You are encouraged to use this file for preparing your statements and to use the information in this file as a Data Section for your answer. Place the statements in the space below the data. The financial statements should be shown in thousands of dollars just as in the Data Section. Goodness Sakes is a privately held company, so earnings per share information is not required.

	6/30/00	6/30/99
Accounts payable (for inventory purchases)	$ 382.4	$ 385.9
Accounts receivable	?	157.9
Accumulated depreciation—building	256.4	236.8
Accumulated depreciation—fixtures	344.8	364.5
Advances from customers	10.5	12.9
Advertising expense	135.5	128.0
Allowance for bad debts	6.3	6.3
Bad debt expense	11.5	15.0
Bonds payable (due 9/1/09)	458.3	258.3
Buildings	583.2	583.2
Cash	56.4	49.4
Common stock	235.2	211.2
Copyrights	10.4	11.2
Cost of goods sold	2,863.9	3,244.0
Depreciation expense	113.9	102.0
Discontinued operations loss (net of tax)	188.3	-0-
Dividends declared on common	100.9	90.0
Dividends declared on preferred	10.6	10.6
Fixtures	894.7	868.5
Gain on sale of old fixtures	54.4	-0-
Goodwill	53.4	56.7
Income tax expense	140.1	20.0
Income tax payable	37.5	50.0
Interest expense	38.8	35.0
Interest payable	7.1	4.7
Inventories	345.1	255.1
Land	100.9	100.9

Long-term notes payable	49.7	60.8
Other operating expenses	345.6	500.0
Paid-in capital in excess of par	180.7	166.7
Preferred stock	132.9	132.9
Prepaid advertising	32.8	42.1
Rent expense	-0-	325.0
Retained earnings (beginning of year)	306.5	269.1
Salaries expense	623.1	714.0
Salaries payable	60.6	55.7
Sales	4,586.6	5,383.0
Short-term investments	133.9	28.0
Short-term notes payable	4.7	13.9
Supplies expense	128.2	162.0
Treasury stock (at cost)	114.1	114.1

Additional information required for the statement of cash flows:

- Goodness sold a large amount of obsolete and worn out fixtures for $64.4. The fixtures originally cost $124.0 and had been depreciated down to a net book value of $10.0.
- Common stock was issued in July. 12,000 shares of common stock were issued in July for $38,000. The par value of the stock is $2 per share.
- Amortization of goodwill and copyrights are included in other operating expenses.
- No bonds were retired during the year. No additional notes payable were issued during the year.
- Short-term investments of $110.0 were made during the year. Goodness also sold $4.1 short-term investments at no gain or loss.

Review the Model-Building Problem Checklist on page 169 to ensure that your model is complete. Use the Print Preview command (File menu) to make sure that the worksheet will print neatly, then print the worksheet. *Check figure: Total assets, $1,692.6.*

To test your model, suppose the auditors made the following three adjustments to the June 30, 2000 balances: sales were reduced by $50,000 to 4,536.6; inventories were increased by $30,000 to 375.1; and accounts payable were increased by $80,000 to 462.4. Record these adjustments to your model. Does your balance sheet still balance? Print the worksheet again. *Check figure: Total assets, $1,722.6.*

Chart (optional)

Using the test data worksheet, create a pie chart showing all major sources of funding for Goodness at year-end: current liabilities, long-term liabilities, and stockholders' equity. Print the chart when done.

	A	B	C	D	E	F	G
2				FINANCL			
3				Financial Statement Preparation			
4							
5				Goodness Sakes Inc.			
6							
7						6/30/00	6/30/99
8	Accounts payable					$382.4	$385.9
9	Accounts receivable					???	157.9
10	Accumulated depreciation - buildings					256.4	236.8
11	Accumulated depreciation - fixtures					344.8	364.5
12	Advances from customers					10.5	12.9
13	Advertising expense					135.5	128.0
14	Allowance for bad debts					6.3	6.3
15	Bad debt expense					11.5	15.0
16	Bonds payable (due 9/1/09)					458.3	258.3
17	Buildings					583.2	583.2
18	Cash					56.4	49.4
19	Common stock					235.2	211.2
20	Copyrights					10.4	11.2
21	Cost of goods sold					2,863.9	3,244.0
22	Depreciation expense					113.9	102.0
23	Discontinued operations loss (net of tax)					188.3	0.0
24	Dividends declared on common					100.9	90.0
25	Dividends declared on preferred					10.6	10.6
26	Fixtures					894.7	868.5
27	Gain on the sale of old fixtures					54.4	0.0
28	Goodwill					53.4	56.7
29	Income tax expense					140.1	20.0
30	Income tax payable					37.5	50.0
31	Interest expense					38.8	35.0
32	Interest payable					7.1	4.7
33	Inventories					345.1	255.1
34	Land					100.9	100.9
35	Long-term notes payable					49.7	60.8
36	Other operating expenses					345.6	500.0
37	Paid in capital in excess of par					180.7	166.7
38	Preferred stock					132.9	132.9
39	Prepaid advertising					32.8	42.1
40	Rent expense					0.0	325.0
41	Retained earnings (beginning of year)					306.5	269.1
42	Salaries expense					623.1	714.0
43	Salaries payable					60.6	55.7
44	Sales					4,586.6	5,383.0
45	Short-term investments					133.9	28.0
46	Short-term notes payable					4.7	13.9
47	Supplies expense					128.2	162.0
48	Treasury stock (at cost)					114.1	114.1
49							

C2 ☆ FINANCIAL ANALYSIS

The following financial information has been abstracted from the 2001 annual report of Zach's Incorporated. Zach's is a traditional department store retailer operating 82 stores under twelve different names. They cater to middle to upper-middle income customers and are widely known for service and value. They offer a wide selection of quality merchandise with special emphasis placed on fashion apparel, accessories, and fashion home furnishings. You have been asked by the company's president and chief operating officer (COO) to use a spreadsheet program to analyze the data and prepare a report for him giving your assessment of Zach's current financial position.

The financial information presented below is accumulated in a file named ANALYSIS on your Student Disk. You are encouraged to use this file for preparing your analysis and to use the information in this file as a Data Section for your answer.

Five-Year Selected Financial Data	2001	2000	1999	1998	1997
Operating Results			(in millions)		
Net sales	$2,367	$2,313	$2,266	$2,156	$2,028
Cost of goods sold	1,671	1,595	1,551	1,476	1,378
Selling, general & admin. exp.	527	502	480	452	432
Provision for relocation		10			
Interest expense	23	23	23	23	24
Interest income	(4)	(4)	(3)	(3)	(3)
Other income	(29)	(26)	(22)	(19)	(18)
Income before income taxes	179	213	237	227	216
Income taxes	55	83	93	98	105
Net income	124	130	144	130	111
Financial Position					
Cash	$ 45	$ 71	$ 87	$ 97	$ 106
Receivables	667	644	625	589	548
Inventories	393	393	362	332	307
Other current assets	12	5	2	2	2
Total current assets	1,117	1,113	1,076	1,020	963
Net property and equipment	445	408	355	310	295
Investments and other assets	35	27	21	23	21
Total assets	1,597	1,548	1,452	1,353	1,279
Total current liabilities	$ 182	$ 240	$ 244	$ 246	$ 275
Long-term debt	241	231	227	235	236
Retained earnings	1,163	1,066	969	861	756
Stockholders' equity	1,174	1,077	981	872	768

Other Data

Capital expenditures for property and equipment	$ 82	$ 97	$ 92	$ 58	$ 64
Depreciation	35	36	37	38	34
Dividends declared and paid	27	34	35	26	21
Number of shares outstanding	37	37	37	37	37
Year-end stock market price*	45	50	93	70	56
Number of stores at year-end*	82	80	80	79	82
Total square feet (thousands)*	12,683	12,077	11,791	11,124	11,105

*not in millions

Quarterly Data

2000	1st Q	2nd Q	3rd Q	4th Q	Total
Sales	$494	$515	$571	$787	$2,367
Income before taxes	42	25	50	62	179
Net income	28	17	34	45	124

2001	1st Q	2nd Q	3rd Q	4th Q	Total
Sales	$478	$505	$555	$775	$2,313
Income before taxes	44	27	56	86	213
Net income	27	16	34	53	130

Industry Statistics

Current ratio, 3.5
Quick ratio, 2.0
Accounts receivable turnover, 8.38
Days' sales in receivables, 44
Inventory turnover, 3.65
Days' sales in inventory, 100
Times-interest earned, 5.2
Asset turnover, 1.66
Return on total assets, 7.67%
Return on equity, 12.09%
Price-earnings ratio, 18
Dividend yield, 2.5%
Dividend payout ratio, 31%
Gross profit (margin) ratio, 38.1%
Profit margin, 2.94%
Long-term debt to equity ratio, .55
Overall debt ratio, 47%

Common size income statement

Sales	100%
Gross profit	38
Income before taxes	7
Net income	3

Common size balance sheet

Cash	6%
Accounts receivable	30
Inventory	27
Property and equipment	37
Current liabilities	18%
Long-term debt	29
Stockholders' equity	53

Monthly sales as a percent of total sales

	Sales
January	5.3%
February	5.8
March	7.4
April	7.4
May	7.8
June	7.4
July	6.7
August	8.1
September	8.0
October	8.2
November	10.7
December	17.2
	100.0%

Selected five-year industry statistics:

	2001	**2000**	**1999**	**1998**	**1997**
Sales per square foot	$248	$193	$219	$206	$178
Sales growth (year-to-year)	9.3%	8.7%	9.3%	8.3%	6.0%

Check off the ratios below that your instructor wants you to include in your report. You will want to group these ratios by type according to your textbook (profitability, liquidity, and so forth). Compute them for all five years. Some ratios require average balances rather than year-end figures. Since figures are not available for 1996, use year-end balances rather than average amounts for 1997 ratios. Zach's has no preferred stock. Your instructor may also provide you with additional ratios or statistics to compute. Enter them at the bottom of each list.

In your analysis, note Zach's current position as well as important trends. Describe changes in profitability, liquidity, long-term solvency, and so forth. Evaluate these changes in light of the future. Compare ratios to industry standards.

Standard Ratios and Statistics

a.   Working capital

b.   Current ratio

c.   Acid test (quick) ratio

d.   Accounts receivable turnover

e.   Number of days' sales in receivables

f.   Inventory turnover

g.   Number of days' sales in inventory

h.   Times-interest-earned

i.   Total asset turnover

j.   Rate of return on total assets

k.   Rate of return on stockholders' equity

l.   Earnings per share

m.   Dividends per share

n.   Price-earnings ratio

o.   Dividend yield

p.   Dividend payout ratio

q.   Gross profit (margin) ratio

r.   Profit margin (net income/sales)

s.   Long-term debt to equity ratio

t.   Overall debt ratio

u.   Book value per share

v.

w.

x.

Trends

a.   Sales

b.   Cost of goods sold

c.   Gross profit

d.   Selling, general and administrative expenses

e.   Income before taxes

f.   Net income

g.

Other

a.   Sales per square foot

b.   Common size income statements (vertical analysis)

c.   Common size balance sheets (vertical analysis)

d.   Statement of cash flows for 1998–2001

e.   Comparative income statements between years 2001 and 2000 (horizontal analysis—compute dollar change and percent change)

f.   Comparative balance sheets between years 2001 and 2000 (horizontal analysis—compute dollar change and percent change)

g.   Seasonal sales and income analysis (only two years available)

h.

Review the Model-Building Problem Checklist on page 169 to ensure that your model is complete and ready to be graded. Use the Print Preview command (File menu) to make sure that the worksheet will print neatly, then print the worksheet. *No check figures are provided.*

No test data is provided for this model.

Chart (optional)

Prepare a 3-D area chart comparing earnings per share and dividends per share over the five-year period. Print the chart when done.

Zach's Inc.

Operating Results	2001	2000	1999	1998	1997
Net sales	$2,367	$2,313	$2,266	$2,156	$2,028
Cost of goods sold	1,671	1,595	1,551	1,476	1,378
Selling, general & admin. exp.	527	502	480	452	432
Provision for relocation		10			
Interest expense	23	23	23	23	24
Interest income	(4)	(4)	(3)	(3)	(3)
Other income	(29)	(26)	(22)	(19)	(18)
Income before income taxes	179	213	237	227	216
Income taxes	55	83	93	98	105
Net Income	124	130	144	130	111

Financial Position	2001	2000	1999	1998	1997
Cash	$45	$71	$87	$97	$106
Receivables	667	644	625	589	548
Inventories	393	393	362	332	307
Other current assets	12	5	2	2	2
Total current assets	1,117	1,113	1,076	1,020	963
Net property and equipment	445	408	355	310	295
Investments and other assets	35	27	21	23	21
Total assets	1,597	1,548	1,452	1,353	1,279
Total current liabilities	$182	$240	$244	$246	$275
Long-term debt	241	231	227	235	236
Retained earnings	1,163	1,066	969	861	756
Stochholders' equity	1,174	1,077	981	872	768

Other Data	2001	2000	1999	1998	1997
Capital expenditures for property & equi	$82	$97	$92	$58	$64
Depreciation	35	36	37	38	34
Dividends declared and paid	27	34	35	26	21
Number of shares outstanding	37	37	37	37	37
Year-end stock market price	$45	$50	$93	$70	$56
Number of stores at year end	82	80	80	79	82
Total square feet	12,683	12,077	11,791	11,124	11,105

2001	1st Q	2nd Q	3rd Q	4th Q	Total
Sales	$494	$515	$571	$787	$2,367
Income before taxes	42	25	50	62	179
Net income	28	17	34	45	124

2000	1st Q	2nd Q	3rd Q	4th Q	Total
Sales	$478	$505	$555	$775	$2,313
Income before taxes	44	27	56	86	213
Net income	27	16	34	53	130

C3 ☼ THREE-MONTH MASTER BUDGET

The balance sheet of Pasciuto Corp. as of June 30, 2000 is as follows:

Pasciuto Corp.
Balance Sheet
June 30, 2000

Assets

Cash		$ 20,850
Accounts receivable		96,000
Raw materials		51,120
Finished goods		32,200
Land		25,000
Plant and equipment	$250,000	
Less: Accumulated depreciation	56,000	194,000
		$419,170

Liabilities and Stockholders' Equity

Accounts payable to suppliers		$ 20,000
Common stock	$ 50,000	
Retained earnings	349,170	399,170
		$419,170

The following information has been extracted from Pasciuto's records:

1.   Pasciuto manufactures and sells Laffs. The company has projected unit sales for its product for the next five months as follows:

	Units
July	7,000
August	8,000
September	10,000
October	8,000
November	7,000

All sales are made on account. Laffs sell for $30 each. Forty percent of all sales are collected in the month of sale. The remaining 60% are collected in the following month.

2.   Management desires to maintain the finished goods inventory for Laffs at 20% of the following month's sales. Pasciuto's June 30, 2000 finished goods inventory consists of 1,400 Laffs.

3. In order to produce one Laff, the following units of raw materials are used:

Raw Material	Units
Bull	5
Winkle	3

The price of Bull has recently risen and is now $2 per unit. The price of Winkle is $1.40 per unit. Management desires to maintain the ending raw materials inventory for both Bull and Winkle at 50% of the following month's production needs. Pasciuto's June 30, 2000 raw material inventory consists of 18,000 units of Bull (@ $2.00 each) and 10,900 units of Winkle (@ $1.40 each).

4. Seventy percent of all purchases are paid in the month of purchase. The remaining 30% are paid in the subsequent month.

5. The company's product requires 30 minutes of direct labor time to complete. All labor costs are paid in the month incurred. Each hour of direct labor costs $12.

6. Factory overhead is applied at the rate of $6 per direct labor hour. Actual overhead costs are paid as they are incurred. Monthly differences between applied and actual overhead costs are expected to be negligible.

7. Selling and administrative expenses are $5,000 per month plus 10% of sales. They are paid in the month incurred.

8. Plant and equipment depreciates at the rate of $6,000 per year. This depreciation is incurred evenly throughout the year and is included in the factory overhead costs mentioned above.

Design a worksheet (file name BIGBUD) for Pasciuto Corp. to prepare the following July, August, and September budgets for 2000: sales budget, production budget, raw materials purchases budget, cash budget, projected unit cost to produce one Laff, budgeted income statement, and budgeted balance sheet. Use a column of the worksheet for each month and a final column for totals for the quarter. Round budget calculations (except unit costs) to the nearest dollar. The sales budget and raw materials purchases budgets should be expressed both in units and dollars. Pasciuto uses FIFO cost flow assumption for valuing inventories.

The acid test for developing this model: When you are done, are your balance sheets in balance?

Review the Model-Building Problem Checklist on page 169 to ensure that your worksheet is complete and ready to be graded. Use the Print Preview command (File menu) to make sure that the worksheet will print neatly, then print the worksheet. *Check figure: Total assets at the end of July, $454,278.*

Increase the price of Laff to $35 to test your model. Does your worksheet calculate throughout, and do your balance sheets balance?

Print the worksheet again. *Check figure: Total assets at the end of July, $485,778.*

Chart (optional)

Using the test data, create a 3-D area chart that compares monthly cash flow (change in the cash account) with monthly net income. Print the chart when done.

	A	B	C	D	E
1					
2			**BIGBUD**		
3			*Three-Month Master Budget*		
4					
5			Pasciuto Corp.		
6			Balance Sheet, June 30, 2000		
7					
8	Cash			$20,850	
9	Accounts receivable			96,000	
10	Raw materials			51,120	
11	Finished goods			32,200	
12	Land			25,000	
13	Plant and equipment		$250,000		
14	Less: accumulated depreciation		56,000	194,000	
15	Total assets			$419,170	
16					
17	Accounts payable to suppliers			$20,000	
18	Common Stock		$50,000		
19	Retained Earnings		349,170	399,170	
20	Total liabilities and equity			$419,170	
21					
22					
23	Budgeted Laff sales in units				
24	July		7,000		
25	August		8,000		
26	September		10,000		
27	October		8,000		
28	November		7,000		
29	Selling price		$30		
30	Collections from customers				
31	Collected in month of sale		40%		
32	Collected the following month		60%		
33	Desired finished goods inventory				
34	(% of next month's unit sales)		20%		
35	Desired raw material inventory				
36	(% of next month's production needs)		50%		
37	Raw material units needed to produce one Laff				
38	Bull		5		
39	Winkle		3		
40	Beginning inventory units & cost				
41	Laff		1,400	$23.00	
42	Bull		18,000	$2.00	
43	Winkle		10,800	$1.40	
44	Purchases				
45	Paid in the month of purchase		70%		
46	Paid in the subsequent month		30%		
47					
48	Direct labor time to produce one Laff		0.5	hours	
49	Cost of direct labor		$12	per hour	
50	Factory overhead		$6	per direct labor hr.	
51					
52	Selling and administrative expenses		$5,000	fixed	
53			10%	variable	
54	Plant and equipment depreciation		$6,000	per year	
55					